"can't overheard talk now."

installation by
Wendy Richmond and Michael Chladil

OVERHEARD

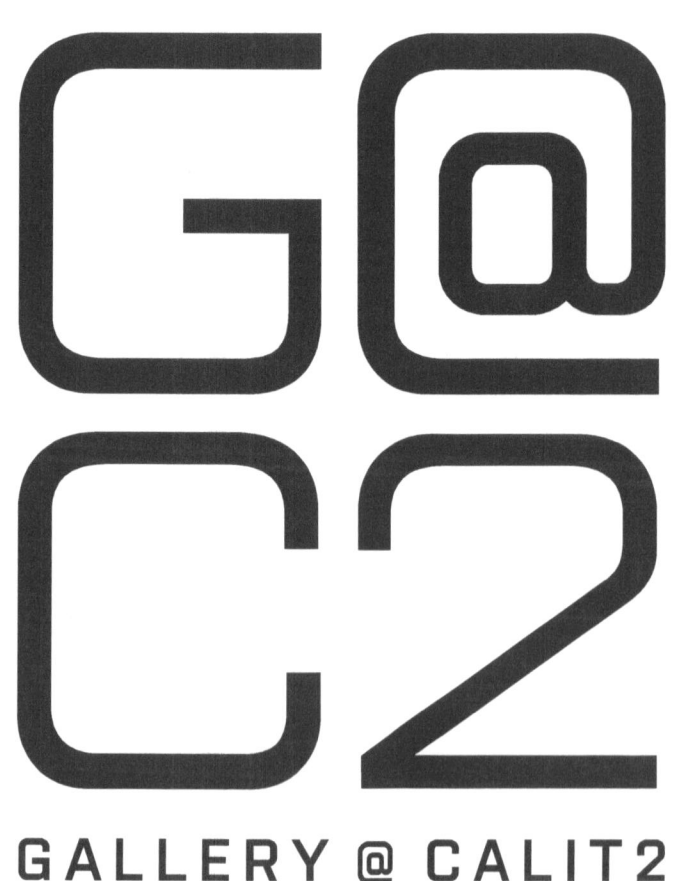

GALLERY @ CALIT2

Published by the gallery@calit2

University of California, San Diego
9500 Gilman Drive
La Jolla, CA, 920093-0436

ISBN 978-0-578-05311-0

GALLERY@CALIT2
EXHIBITION CATALOG N°8

OVERHEARD

GALLERY INSTALLATION
JANUARY 15, 2010 TO MARCH 12, 2010

CONTENTS

INTRODUCTION

BY WENDY RICHMOND

"Wherever we are, what we hear is mostly noise. When we ignore it, it disturbs us. When we listen to it, we find it fascinating." —John Cage, The Future of Music: Credo

On a recent winter day in a New York City café, my fellow coffee drinkers and I were the captive audience of a woman speaking loudly into her cell phone. "Don't worry, he'll be fine. He's not, like, doubled over or anything." Then she made a few more calls, essentially repeating the same thing. During her conversations, this woman was deeply ensconced in her private bubble, and yet an entire café full of people was in on the news.

We all overhear snippets of cell phone conversations. Some are tender ("Where have you been? I was worried!"), some are classically mundane ("I'm on the corner. Where are you?"), and some are just plain annoying ("Hello? Can you hear me? Can you hear me? Hello?"). And we all know that each one of us has spoken those very same phrases.

Twenty-first century city dwellers simultaneously occupy and retreat from public space: we create private bubbles—using personal technology like iPods, cell phones, and laptops—to serve as a buffer zone. But often, the more we retreat, the more we reveal. By withdrawing into the bubble, that is, losing ourselves within our private, self-made spaces, we are simultaneously exposing more to the people around us.

In Jane Jacobs's seminal book, *The Death and Life of Great American Cities*, she wrote, "Privacy is precious in cities. It is indispensable. Perhaps it is precious and indispensable everywhere, but most places, you cannot get it. In small settlements, everyone knows your affairs. In the city, everyone does not—only those you choose to tell will know much about you."

A lot has changed since Jacobs wrote these words. Have we abdicated our privacy by creating our ever more robust personal bubbles? Are we no longer choosing what to tell and to whom we will tell it?

How does our personal technology affect the ways we occupy, experience and participate in public spaces? Do we use personal technology as a form of retreat—intentional or not—from the physical, public space?

The exhibit "Overheard" studies this changing landscape by exploring halves of cell phone conversations, all overheard (and copied down) in the density of midtown Manhattan. The personalities are students, tourists, health care workers, out-of-work interviewees, entrepreneurs, dads and moms, sons and daughters.

These fragments of half-conversations have become the content for the installation "Overheard." Gallery visitors enter a darkened space. Scattered about the room are twenty small, glowing digital monitors, which display fragments of conversations. As the visitors walk into the room, they hear a series of audio phrases and see large, constantly changing video projections of typography that fill the walls. In addition, there are two interactive "rope&pulley" systems, which visitors can "play" to control aspects of the voices and typographic projections. Phrases of words become choreographic—stretching and shrinking, overlapping and collapsing in on themselves. Depending on the length of time a visitor stays in the gallery, the experience will range from quiet and dark to cacophonous and intensely visual.

Urban dwellers are under a constant barrage of aural and visual cacophony, as both participants and observers. Our goal in this exhibit is to create a rich visual and aural space that undergoes constant change depending on the visitors' action and inaction. The experience in this space will hopefully linger as the visitors re-enter their normal routines. As John Cage proposed, the noise of the everyday world, which can be so disturbing, can also become fascinating.

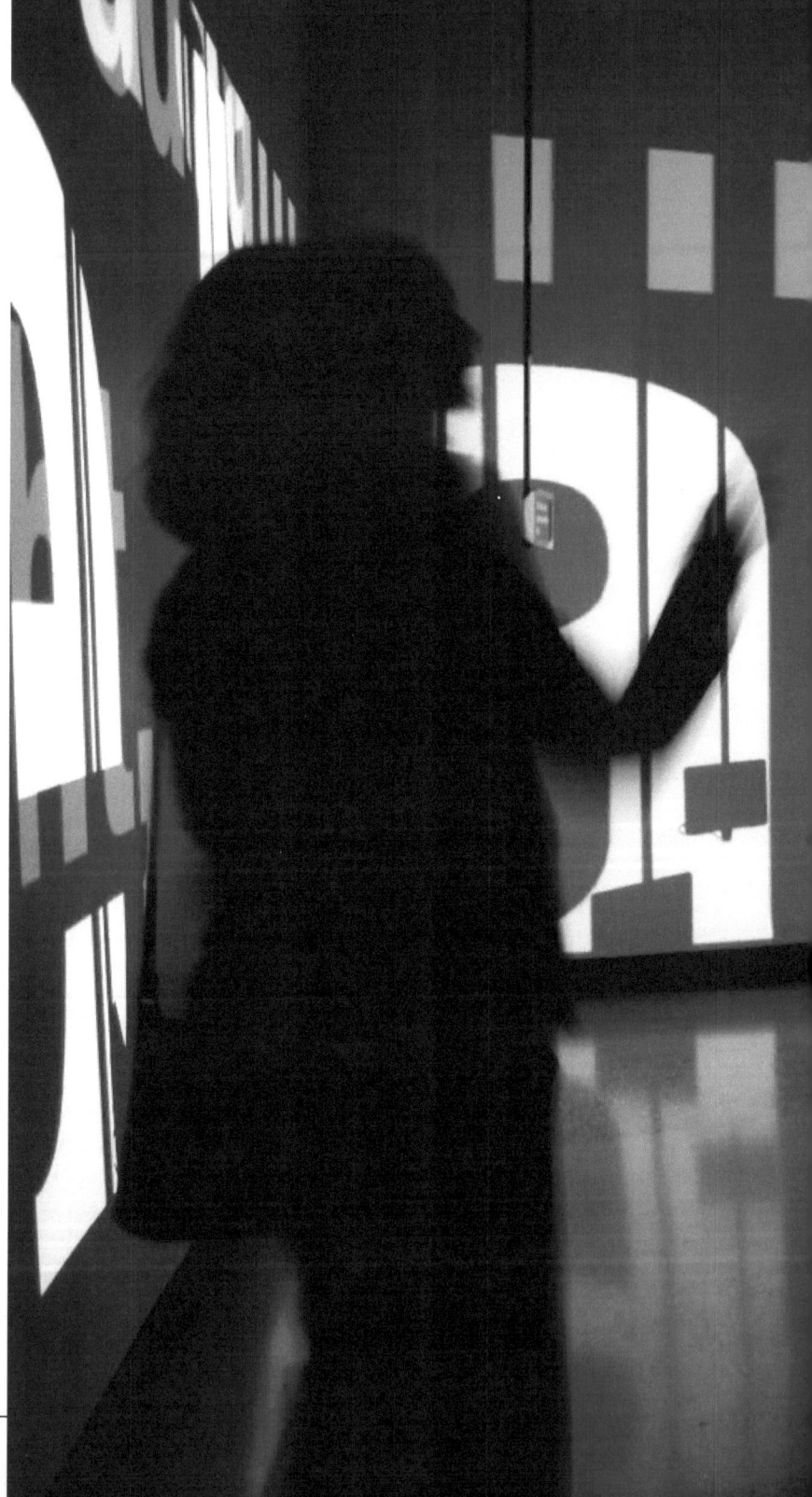

If we don't get the check today,

I can't keep eating out like this.

and then at each time

INTERVIEW

BY SUSAN HODARA*

---

*SUSAN HODARA** is a freelance journalist who writes frequently about the arts. Her work has appeared in The New York Times, Communication Arts, Harvard Magazine, Wesleyan Magazine and other publications. She is also a memoirist whose pieces are published in anthologies and literary journals. She is currently collaborating on a memoir about mothers, daughters and women working together. www.susanhodara.com.

Several months before the opening of "Overheard," the artists Wendy Richmond and Michael Chladil were immersed in the creative process, experimenting with the components of their upcoming exhibition.

Wendy is an artist, author and educator whose work investigates the overlap of public and private space in the 21st century. Her exhibition, "Public Privacy: Wendy Richmond's Surreptitious Cellphone," was first shown at the Museum of Photographic Arts in San Diego in 2007. Her latest book, Art Without Compromise*, was released in October. She has written "Design Culture," her column in Communication Arts magazine, since 1984.

Michael, a musician and an engineer with a particular interest in prototyping, interned with Wendy from 2007 to 2008, while he was a graduate student in the Interactive Telecommunications Program at New York University. They explored their mutual interests in two areas: the creative process and the effects of juxtaposing visual and aural elements with physicality.

With "Overheard," Wendy moves from the visual image into the realm of text and audio. The show also extends her working relationship with Michael. They sat down to share their thoughts about their intentions, their challenges, the larger context of the work, and what gallery-goers might hope to experience.

SUSAN HODARA [SH]: Describe "Overheard."

Wendy Richmond [WR]: "Overheard" is a multimedia exhibit consisting of projected text and audio that appear in varying degrees from silence to cacophony. The material is based on overheard cellphone conversations that I collected over several years in a Starbucks near the apartment where I lived in midtown Manhattan. Like my prior work with surreptitious cellphone videos, its underlying theme is public privacy.

SH: You worked collaboratively on the creation of this exhibit. How did "Overheard" come to be, and what were your respective roles?

WR: When I was asked by Calit2 to present an exhibit at gallery@calit2, I recognized a two-pronged opportunity. First, it provided a deadline to complete the body of work I was already working on, focusing on overheard cellphone conversations. Secondly, the exhibit presented a chance to create a concrete show-able project with Michael, with whom I'd been collaborating on conceptual work for a couple of years.

Michael Chladil [MC]: My role is the toolmaker. I make the technology that allows Wendy to do her experimentation. It means listening to her and then translating what she wants, and also anticipating what she might need. For example, Wendy said she wanted to have multiple layers of conversations and sounds. There were a number of ways I could have provided that, but the way I chose was to set up a system that would allow me to adjust the parameters of the sound without having to go back and edit the sounds themselves.

WR: What's becoming more and more apparent to me is that Michael understands the way I work, not just because we've worked together for a long time, but because it's his natural way, too. I don't want to know exactly what's going to happen in this exhibit. What I want is a palette of elements that we like and that work, but also the ability to move stuff around, play with it, see what can happen. Michael's tools inherently give me the flexibility to see things I might never have thought of trying. I enjoy the surprises I am able to get from working with him.

SH: What does "Overheard" entail?

WR: Let's talk about it in terms of the elements involved. First we have the components, which are visual, aural and interactive. Visually, we have huge projected typography and digital eight-by-ten-inch screens that display text. Aurally, we have recorded voice and sound. And we have Michael's rope&pulley, which allows visitors physical interaction. Next are our tools, which are the delivery system. The tools are the pieces of technology that Michael has developed, and the equipment necessary to use them, like computers, projectors and speakers.

MC: The tools are the combination of what I write and the environment I'm writing in, which is the programming language Max/MSP/Jitter. The graphical nature of this language allows me to sketch ideas quickly and revise them later, which is very important for our process.

WR: We also have our palette, which are the permutations that we — and, in some cases, gallery-goers — can play with. These include the size, spacing and transparency of the typography, the loudness and direction of the sound and the number of simultaneous visual and aural projections.

MC: With the rope&pulley, it's the mappings of the action users take when they're pulling and what it affects. That's part of the palette.

WR: And then there's the content, which is what the show is about. In "Overheard," the content is overheard cellphone conversations and sharing public space.

SH: Talk more about the content in "Overheard."

WR: I think it's true for a lot of artists that they don't totally know what a body of work is about until it's done, and maybe until it's been around for a while. But they do have an intention.

A lot of my work is about public privacy, and asks the question: How do urban dwellers share public space when each of us is alone in our private bubble? If you live in the city, you see this all the time — people packed tightly together, but alone in their private space. I've found this really interesting to observe. My last body of work was observing it visually, through surreptitious cellphone videos. In this work I'm observing it from an aural perspective.

MC: We've been leaving the public sphere since 1979, when Sony introduced the first Walkman, and we've been invading the public space since the early '70s, when people were carrying around boom boxes.

WR: Yeah, I wrote about that in my book, in

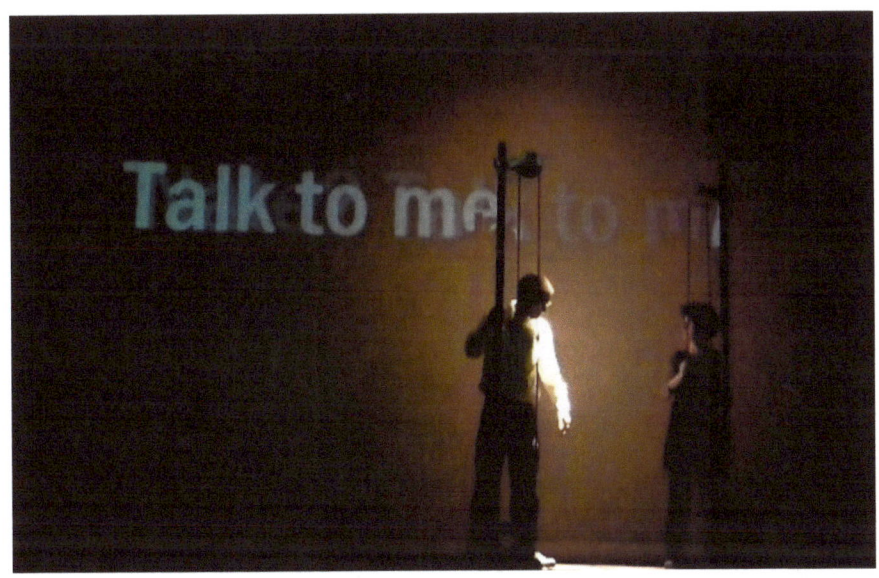

the chapter called "The Internal Retreat from Public Space." I'm fascinated by the role personal technology plays in the way we share dense public space. Before, our private bubble was just staring off into the distance and thinking. In contemporary society, our individual bubbles have been exacerbated, or intensified, by all our little devices — our iPods, cellphones, BlackBerrys, laptops. Then there's the Starbucks phenomenon — people going into crowded cafés with their laptops and their headphones and working in public in their little bubbles. We can get to a point where we're totally unaware of the space that we're in. We travel to a distant land. My intention is observing this interesting phenomenon that is around us all the time, that we get pissed at, that we ignore, that we complain about — and then that we turn around and do ourselves.

SH: Unlike your previous exhibits, "Overheard" contains no images. Why?

WR: Yes, it's all type and sound. There are no pictures. When you're on a cellphone, you're in a weird non-space where you go to the mind's eye. In the exhibit, when you just see text and hear snippets of conversations, you begin to imagine. How is this person dressed? How old? You want to picture who's talking. You try to fill in the gaps. That's an important part of this exhibit — the pieces that are missing, that you don't see and hear.

SH: Talk more about the rope&pulley.

MC: The rope&pulley in its most basic form is a way of manipulating digital content by moving it forward and backward. In "Overheard," we are using it to manipulate projected text and sound interactively. I created the rope&pulley for my Master's thesis at New York University. It was developed for a different purpose: to satisfy an urge to move with music.

WR: One of the things that attracted me to the rope&pulley is that you have to move with it. At a certain point in my career, I reached a point where I was really annoyed at the limited physicality of the computer.

MC: And I feel the same way. It's not overtly stated, but we share this common irritant. It's another reason Wendy and I work well together.

WR: To put it in a more positive light, it was the desire to do something more physical with technology. I like technology, and I like movement, and what I love about the rope&pulley is the physicality of how you interact with it. The way we work with personal technology today — cellphones, BlackBerrys and so forth — sometimes it comes down to just our thumbs. With the rope&pulley, I love the idea that you have to haul away.

MC: It's mostly oak, and the rope is dynamic

climbing rope that was donated by a climbing gym. It feels better than the rope I bought at the hardware store. The rope&pulley was designed using a computer. I crafted the initial versions out of cardboard to get the function, and then had the pieces milled. I assembled them myself.

WR: In "Overheard," the rope&pulley is the vehicle for physical interaction. It lets you play with the conversations. You can make the words move slower or faster; you can make the sounds louder or softer. You can run it in reverse. When you play, you see new stuff. It's fun!

Also, playing with the rope&pulley lets you abstract the conversations so that you listen to them more carefully.

MC: And there's another side to this. The rope&pulley is a content creation system. You could probably make a show that looked like "Overheard" using a few DVD players and projectors. What's different about the rope&pulley is that it's a real-time tool. It's a workflow tool for doing these kinds of things as rapidly as you can think about them.

WR: To clarify, the rope&pulley serves two functions. One is its role in the gallery, and the other is its use when Michael and I are working together. It lets me say: what about this, what about that, what about this, and boom boom boom boom boom, I can see it. If I wanted to see what those ideas looked like using, say, Keynote, well... forget it. In that sense, the rope&pulley is a way for Michael to help me experiment with what we want to show.

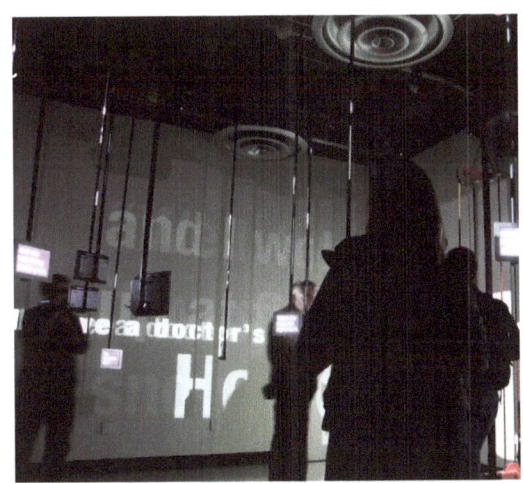

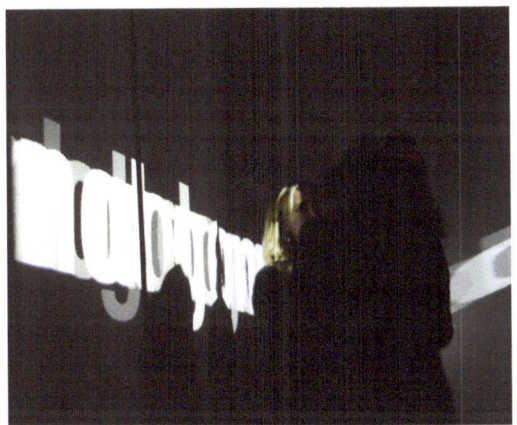

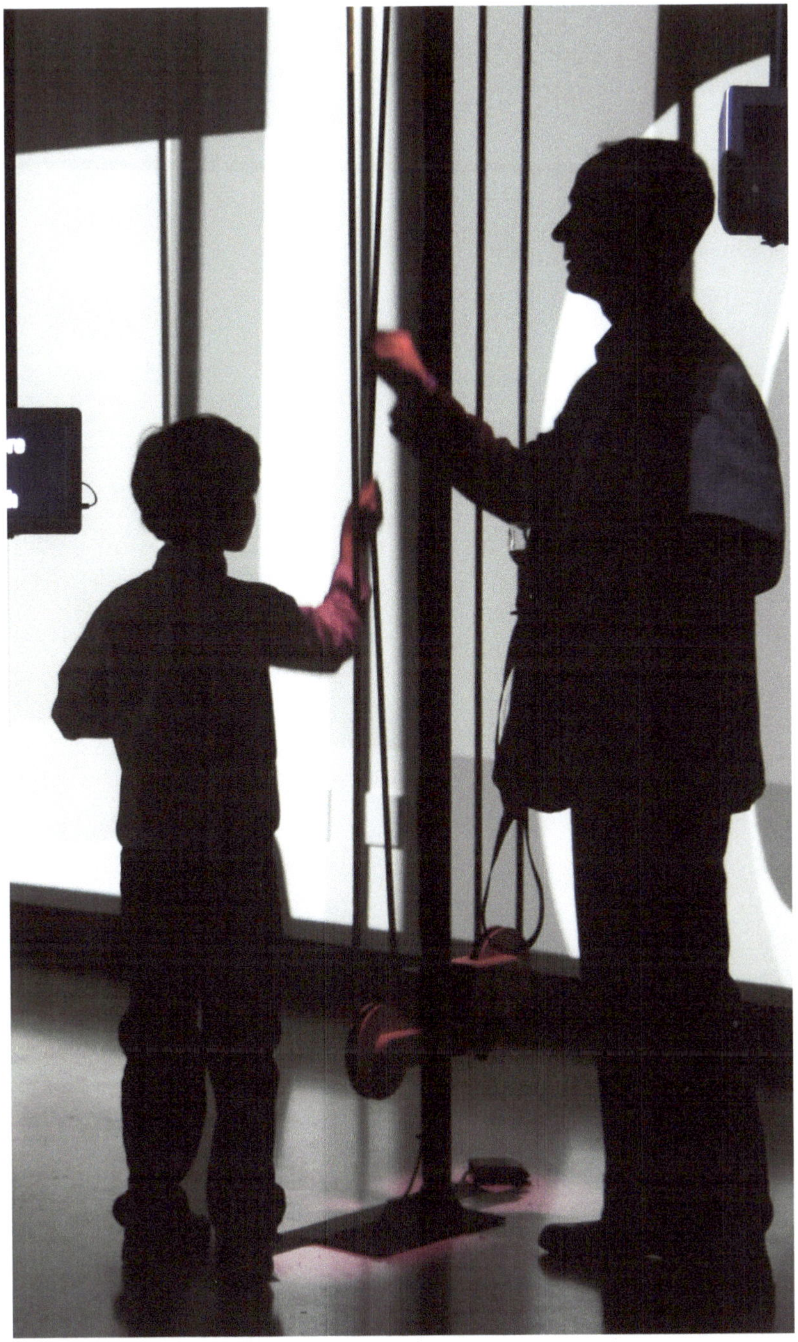

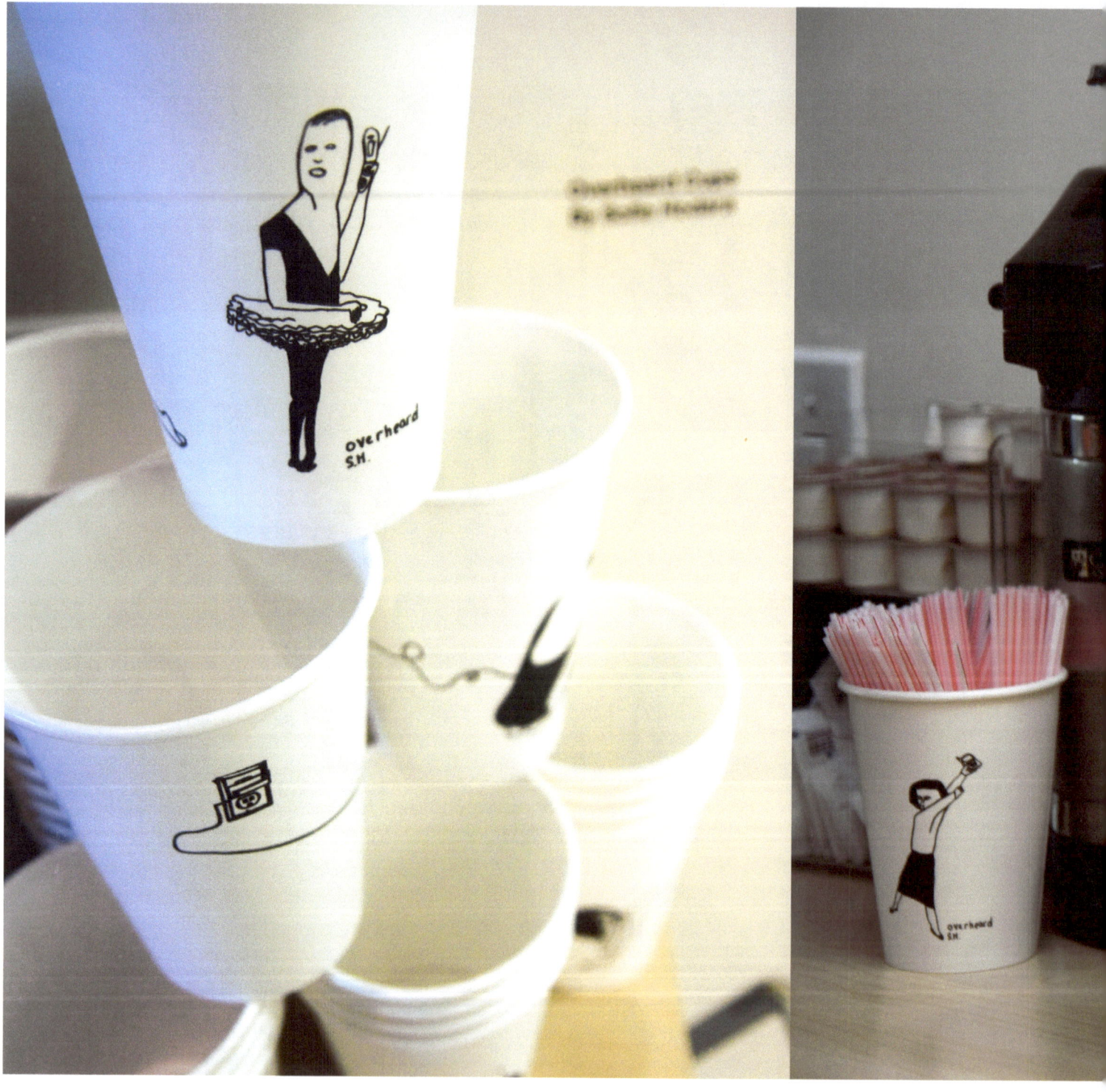

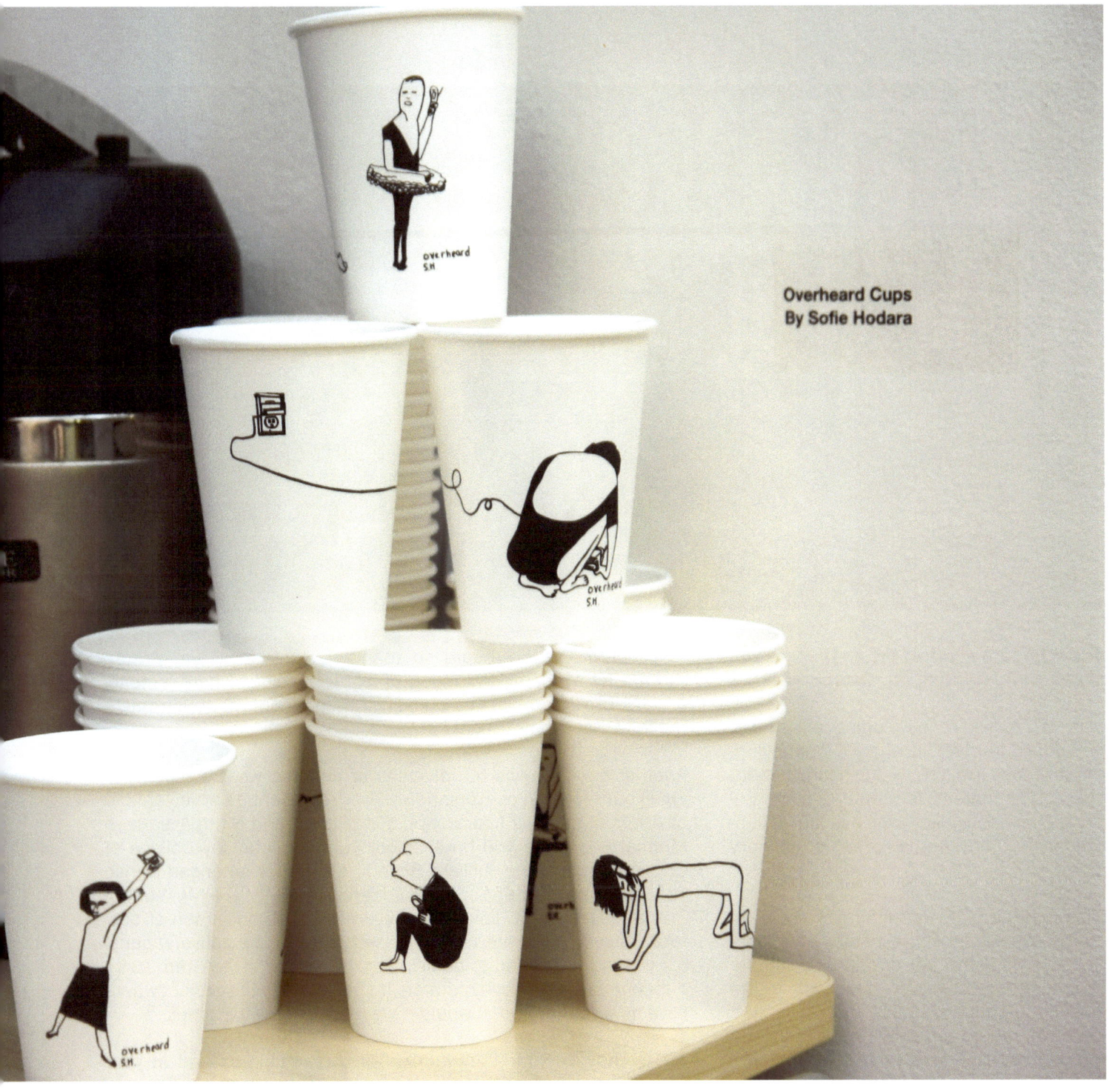

Overheard Cups
By Sofie Hodara

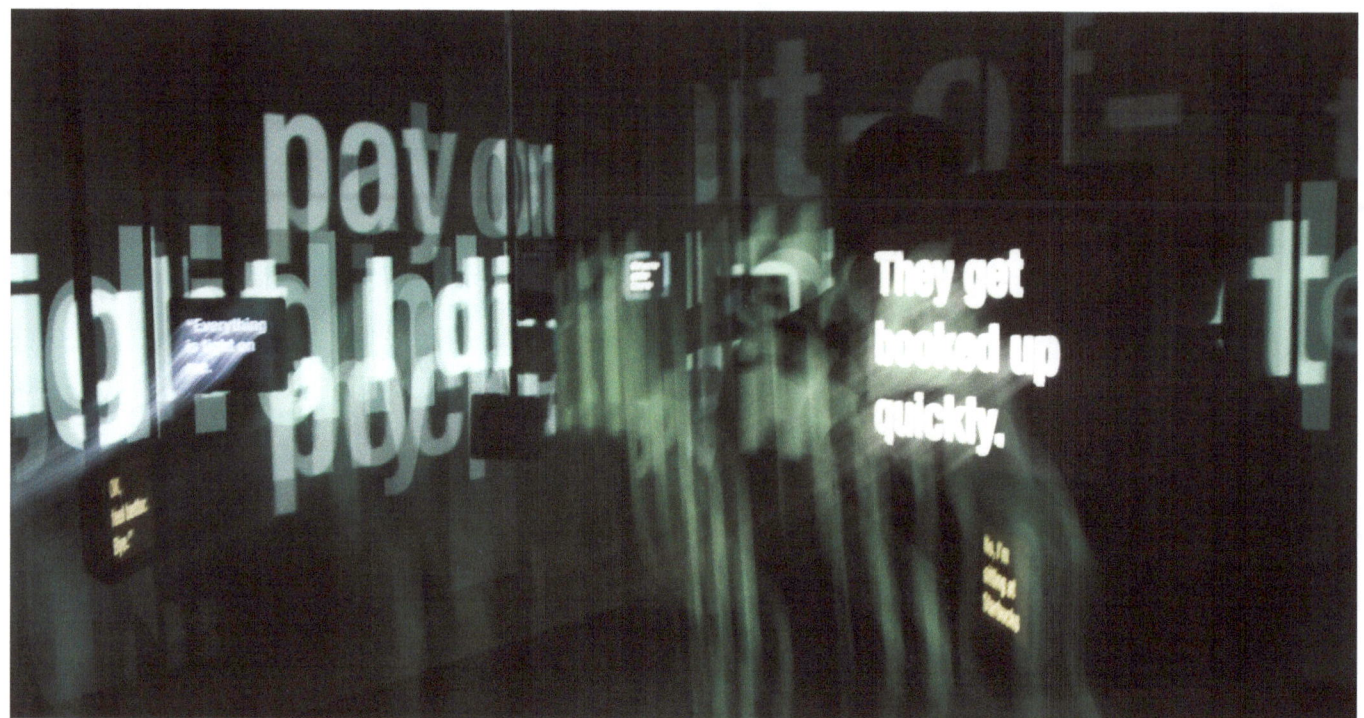

SH: What are some of the challenges you faced while working on "Overheard"?

WR: When you're developing an exhibit, you get so involved in what you're making, what it looks like, that you can forget about the actual content. Is it entertaining? Besides the rope&pulley, which is fun and engaging, is there drama? What is the story here?

This is not a play, with characters who interact. We are presenting snippets of conversations. Some are dramatic; someone is talking about a loved one being in the hospital. Others are quite mundane: "I'm on 58th. Where are you?" We had to ask: Do people respond to more dramatic con-versations? I've overheard so many conversations and written down a lot of them, and much of what is included here is deliberately less dramatic. I've chosen the comments that you might make yourself tomorrow.

Another concern was the diversity of cultures we are representing in our recorded conversations. They represent a particular kind of diversity that you find around 59th Street and Ninth Avenue in Manhattan, where you have Lincoln Center, John Jay College of Criminal Justice, the Juilliard School, Alvin Ailey American Dance Theater, Time Warner Center, Fordham University, the Museum of Arts and Design, St. Luke's-Roosevelt Hospital, and a ton of doctors' offices. There are bits of those places in the conversations. It's where I happened to be living at the time. It's the Starbucks I happened to go to each morning. If I had started the project where I live now, in Brooklyn, it would have been entirely different.

SH: Wendy, in your Communication Arts columns and in your

new book, Art Without Compromise*, you write a lot about the creative process. Can you discuss how your thoughts about the creative process came into play in the development of "Overheard"?

WR: Yes, I am probably more interested in the process than the product, particularly in how not to smother creative seeds. It's about how to maintain a balance between remaining in a state of not knowing all the answers when you're working on a project, and moving forward toward a final product. You want to stay open as long as you can, because if you decide too early what your end result is going to be, you will go down that path, things will become more and more precious, and eventually you'll look back and say, Damn, I didn't even try this and that.

And there's another part of it, which I call "setting up and letting go." You do need your tools and your direction, but if you are rigid, if you insist on knowing exactly where you're going to end up, and you resist experimentation because it might not work, then why bother at all? I want to be surprised. I want to learn from my work.

MC: I came at it a little differently. I was tired of the way I had been working corporately, where we'd spend a lot of time on the design of our products, but ultimately, at the end of the process, it was always a letdown. We knew there were flaws in what we had made, but we had no chance to correct them because they had to be shipped. I wanted to be working on something that didn't have that letdown feeling at the end, when the majority of the feedback was about what was wrong with the product. I'm not interested in the creative process

solely from the perspective of becoming an artist. I'm interested in being able to self-direct my work when the opportunity presents itself, and in being able to enjoy the process of creating.

WR: Even when you are creating art, you are creating a product. I call this the "Creative Process Loop:" Observe, reflect, articulate. Observe, reflect, articulate. You go through iterations.

SH: In creating "Overheard," what mattered most to you?

MC: For me there were two aspects. Making things is of paramount importance to me, and what matters most is that what I am making gets used. Only then can I understand how it needs to be refined so that it gets better. The second part is the safety net offered by working on this show with Wendy — experiencing the creative process that we talked about and that I wanted to learn about, but not going through it by myself.

WR: This show let me live out the theories I believe in, particularly maintaining the balance between knowing and not knowing. We did very specific things that forced us to observe, reflect and articulate — to follow those actual stages. They were useful. Playing out these theories was very important to me.

What also matters so much is that there is joy in the process. I know it's going to be painful. I know it's going to get stressful. I know I'm going to be worried. But there has to be joy. Those moments of beauty and surprise that we come upon unexpect-

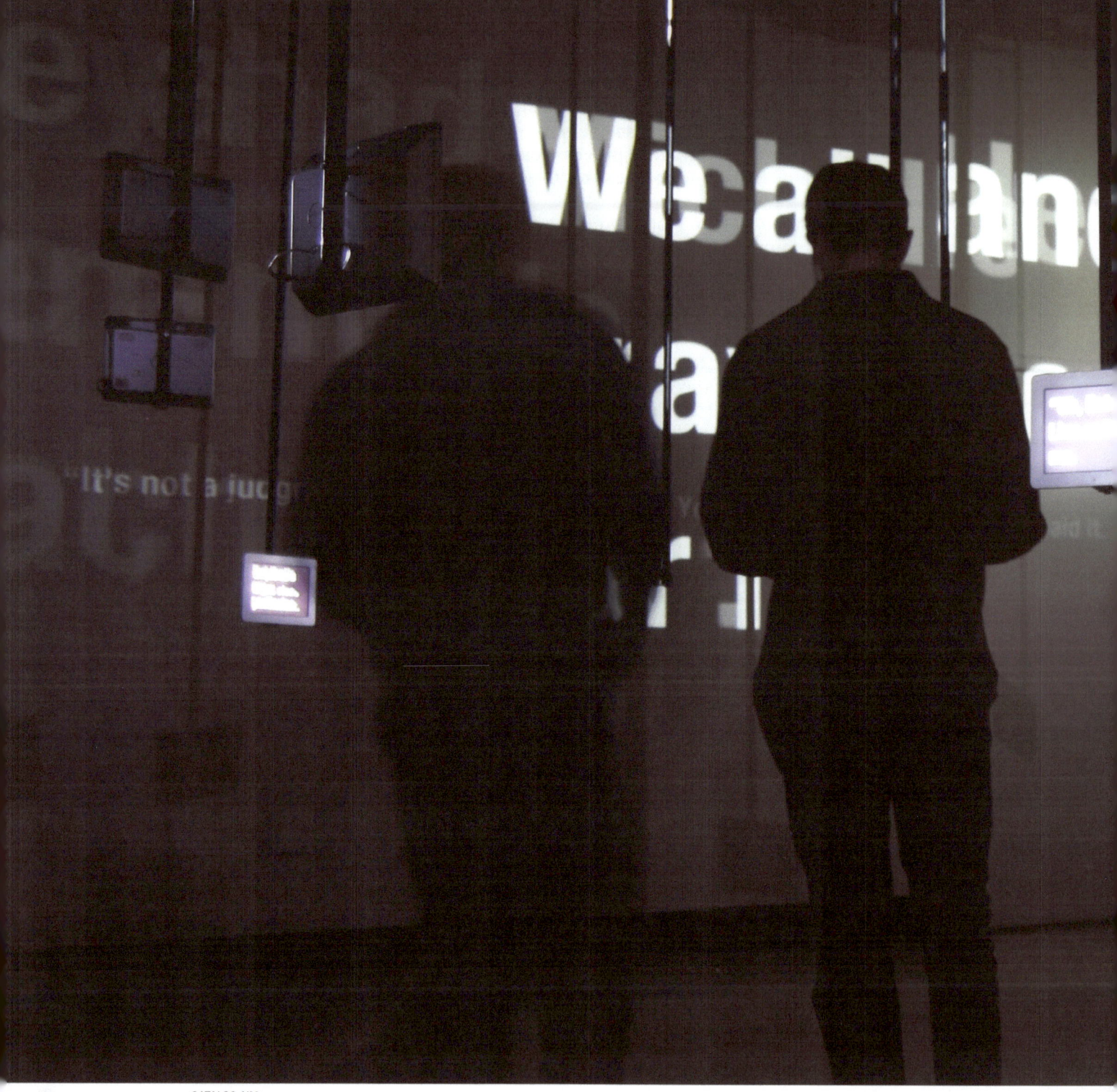

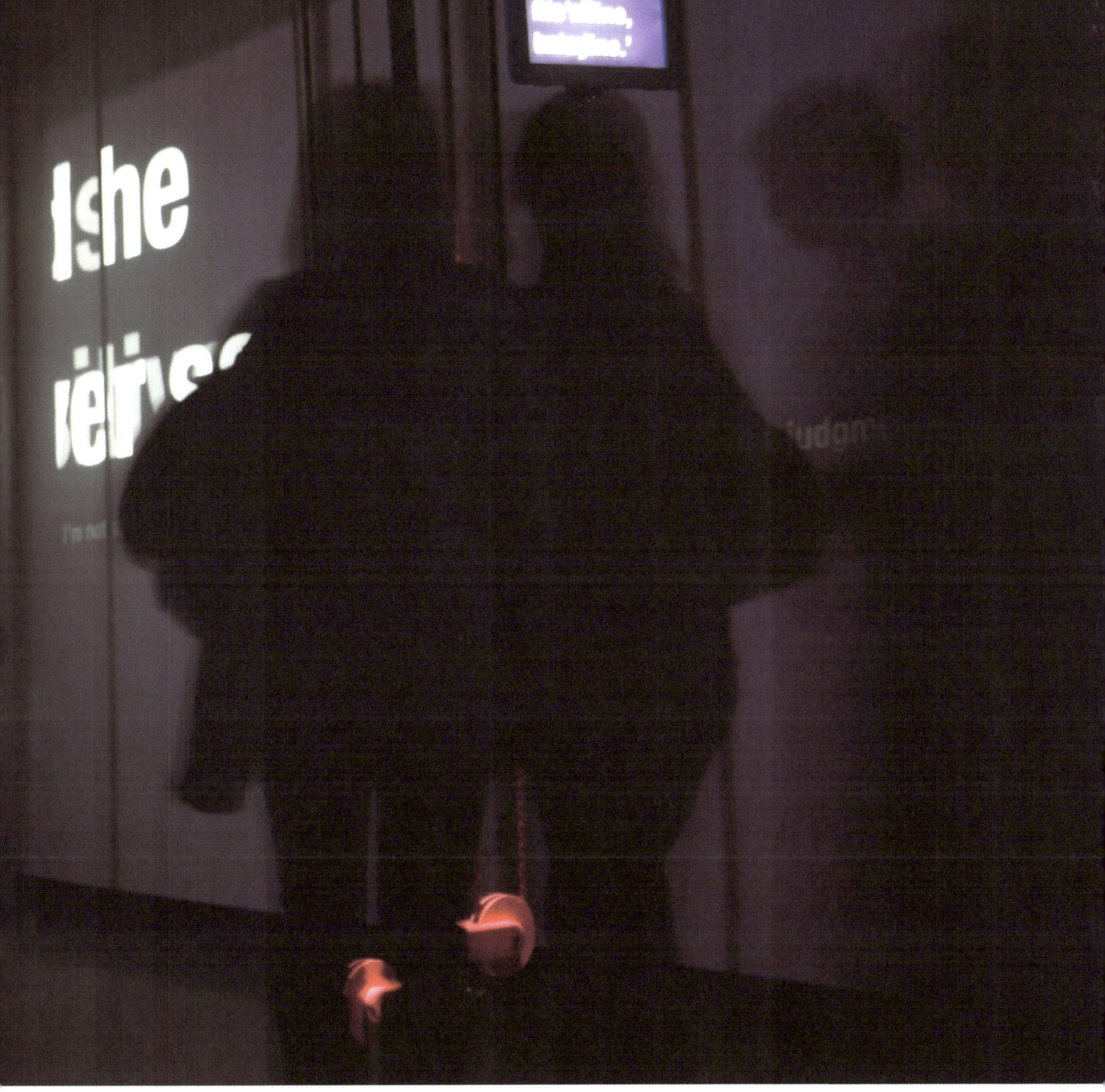

edly — making the exhibit is the excuse for them.

SH: What matters most to you about the end result, the exhibit that is "Overheard?"

MC: It has to work. And I mean more than technically, because that can be unsatisfying in itself. It has to work culturally, too, in the context of what it is.

WR: For me, what's most important is that the show is engaging in many ways. It should be beautiful to look at, and fun to play with, and hopefully it makes people think.

SH: Describe the experience that gallery-goers will have.

WR: It depends. It will be different for everyone, which is great. They will watch, they will listen, they will play. There will be times when it's quiet and not much is going on, and then there will be more and more overlapping visuals and voices and sounds. The experience provides a range between silence in the visual and aural sense, and utter cacophony. And I will throw in one more thing that pertains to the rope&pulley: there will be silence in terms of interaction, and cacophony in terms of interaction.

What I like about being in the gallery for a certain amount of time is that you will hear a voice alone, then you will hear that voice with other voices, and maybe catch it again alone later, or hear a different part of the conversation. Because of the repetition, you start to develop a familiarity with some of the conversations and a relationship with certain characters.

And unexpected things happen. You might see one phrase on a screen that connects to a completely different conversation that you hear. The longer you stay in the gallery, the more layers you'll experience, and the more you'll create your own show. I hope that visitors will become more aware of the layers they experience in their own lives. After they leave, they'll hear what they always hear, but they'll do a double-take and think, I hear this all the time and I never noticed it before.

I love you,
I love you,
I love you.

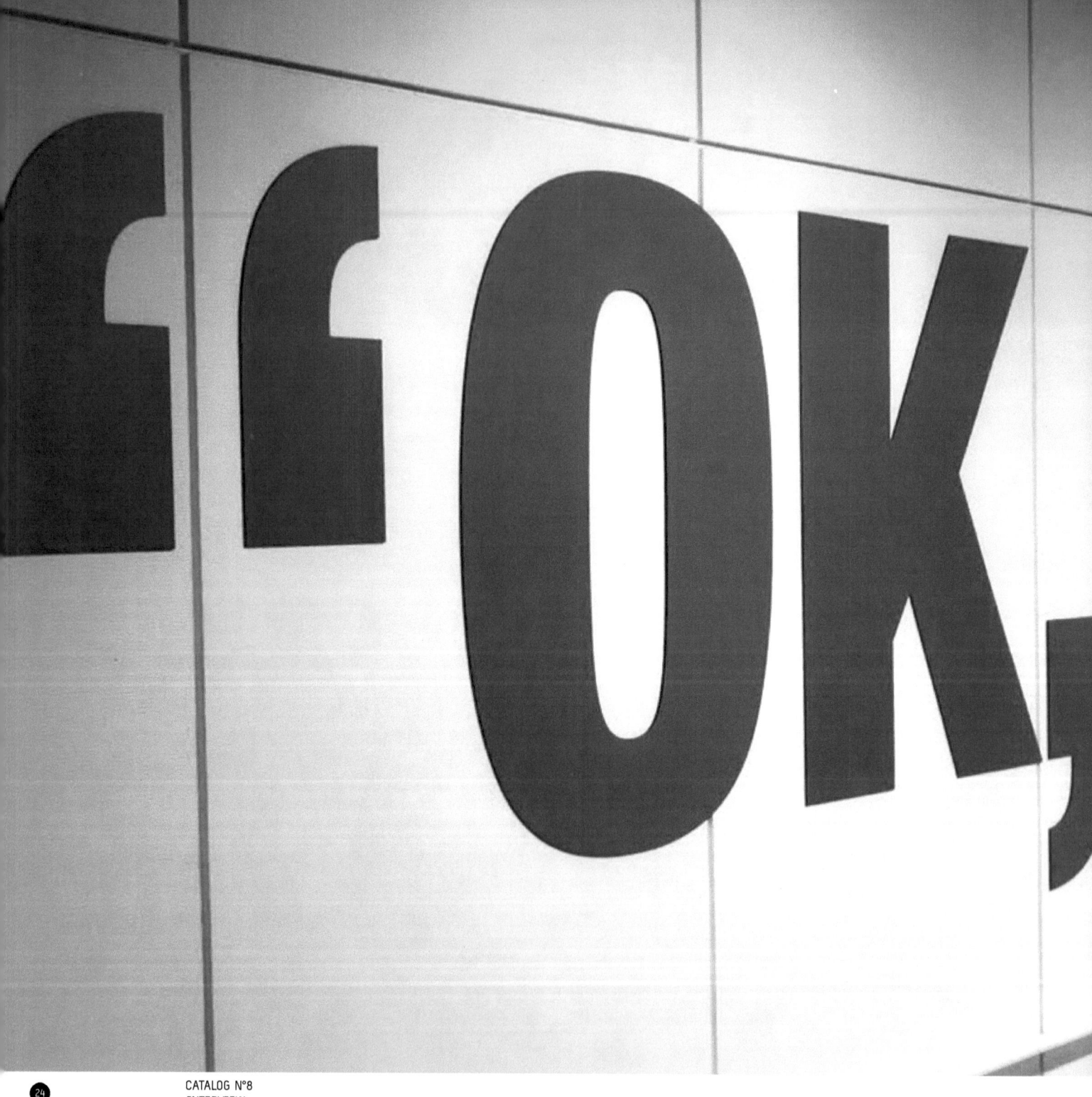

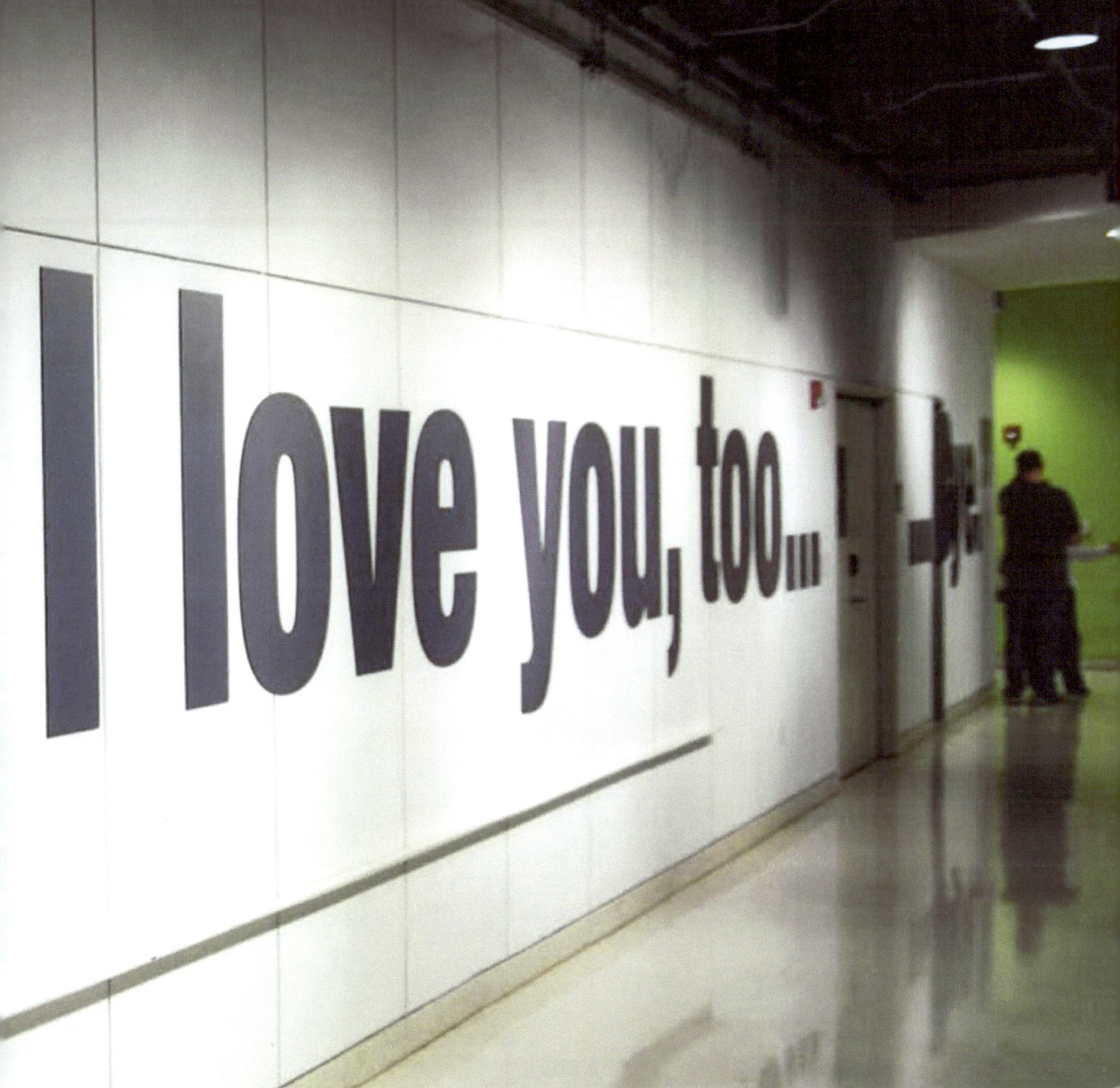

ARTIST BIOGRAPHY

WENDY RICHMOND

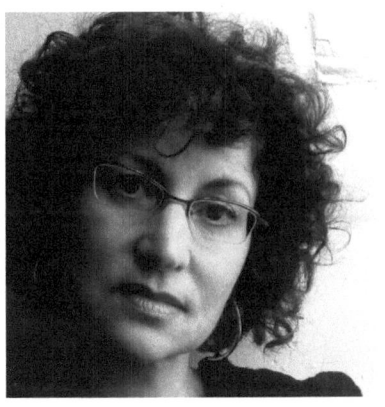

Wendy Richmond is a visual artist, writer and educator whose work explores issues of personal privacy, technology and creativity in contemporary culture. After graduating from Wesleyan University, and with a background in fine arts, design and dance, Richmond began mixing traditional media with new technology at MIT's Visible Language Workshop. She collaborated with programmers to develop pioneering work with interactive books at MIT's Media Lab, and co-founded the Design Lab at WGBH in Boston. She received her Master's degree at New York University. Her teaching experience includes MIT, International Center of Photography and Harvard University Graduate School of Education, where she co-created courses in media and expression.

Richmond is a contributing editor at *Communications Arts* magazine; her regular column "Design Culture" began in 1984. She is the author of *Design & Technology: Erasing the Boundaries* and *overneath*, a collaboration of photography and dance. Her book *Art without Compromise** was published in late 2009 by Allworth Press.

Richmond's photographs, videos, installations and collaborative works have been exhibited internationally. She is the recipient of a Rockefeller Foundation Bellagio Center residency, a National Endowment for the Arts grant, a LEF Foundation grant, the Hatch Award for Creative Excellence, and numerous art and design awards. Richmond's solo exhibition "Public Privacy: Wendy Richmond's Surreptitious Cellphone" was first shown at the Museum of Photographic Arts in San Diego and was featured in the New York Times. It was also presented at the International Association of Privacy Summit in Washington, D.C. and Carroll and Sons in Boston. Richmond is currently collaborating on an interdisciplinary theater work in New York titled "Talk Soon."

Richmond's most recent body of work is "Overheard." When Calit2 commissioned Richmond to create an installation of this work, she invited media artist/interaction designer Michael Chladil to collaborate, and they developed an interactive installation of sound, sight and physicality.

www.wendyrichmond.com

ART / DESIGN

"Personal and personable—a first-hand account of the essentials of the creative process, written in an indomitable and penetrating voice and style."
—Nicholas Negroponte, cofounder, MIT Media Lab; founder and chairman, One Laptop per Child

"Reading Wendy Richmond is like a conversation with a wise friend. The topic of art and its place in our lives is something we have all thought about; it's just that she has thought about it more usefully and can explain her ideas with a jargon-free clarity that is an art in itself."
—Matthew Carter, type designer

"Richmond is absorbed by life and so aware of what is happening around her that she is compelled to make a mental note of it and then speculate later on its significance. Her insights are ironically drawn from the opposite kind of awareness: outsight. Outsight means 'the ability to see and understand external things clearly.' Richmond's ability to observe and derive is what feeds these chapters."
—Chris Pullman, artist; former vice president for design, WGBH Boston

*Art Without Compromise** will inspire artists to change the way they think about their creative landscapes, from personal goals to cultural influences to technological realities. Author Wendy Richmond helps artists to look closely at what they see every day, both in their own art-making and in the world around them. Readers will learn to develop an uncompromising commitment to finding and protecting their own unique process for making their strongest art.

This thought-provoking book covers such topics as:
• understanding the artist's unique identity in relation to the larger culture
• building systems of support and collaboration
• explaining how an artist's needs can lead to innovation and authenticity
• responding to the Internet and changing concepts of what is public and private
• accepting digression as a creative necessity

Artists will come away with a clearer perspective of their past and future work, a critical eye for personal relevance, and an abundance of inspiration.

WENDY RICHMOND began mixing traditional media with new technology at MIT and cofounded the Design Lab at WGBH in Boston. Her teaching experience includes Harvard University Graduate School of Education, School of the Museum of Fine Arts, and International Center of Photography. Richmond is the recipient of a Rockefeller Foundation Bellagio Center residency, a National Endowment for the Arts grant, a LEF Foundation grant, and the Hatch Award for Creative Excellence. She has also served on the national board of AIGA. Richmond has a regular column in *Communication Arts* magazine and is the author of *Design & Technology: Erasing the Boundaries* and *overneath*, a collaboration of photography and dance. She lives in New York City.

Published by Allworth Press
www.allworth.com
Cover design by Wendy Richmond

$24.95/$29.95 Canada

$24.95
ISBN 978-1-58115-666-9
52495>

9 781581 156669

Richmond

ART WITHOUT COMPROMISE*

ART
WITHOUT
COMPROMISE*

Wendy Richmond

In her book *Art Without Compromise**, Wendy Richmond encourages artists to look closely at what they see every day, both in their own art-making and in the world around them. This book covers such topics as: understanding the artist's unique identity in relation to the larger culture; building systems of support and collaboration; explaining how an artist's needs can lead to innovation and authenticity; responding to the Internet and changing concepts of what is public and private; and accepting digression as a creative necessity. Readers come away with a new perspective about their creative landscapes, from personal goals to cultural influences to technological realities.

ARTIST BIOGRAPHY

MICHAEL CHLADIL

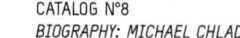

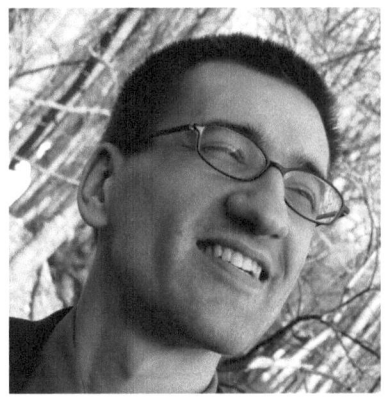

Michael Chladil is an interaction designer, prototyping consultant, and multimedia artist who grew up playing with computers, pianos, and small power tools. While a student at Stevens Institute of Technology he created codeBLUE: a prototype wireless, interactive dance-club system sponsored by Telcordia Technologies, which allowed people with limited musical abilities to experience group musical improvisation. As a student employee of the newly renovated DeBaun Auditorium at the school, he brought professional-quality digital multi-track playback and recording technology to the campus for the first time and continued in his later role as Resident Sound Designer to upgrade the technical capabilities of the facility.

A pent-up desire to build physical interactive musical systems led Chladil to earn a Master's degree at the Interactive Telecommunications Program (ITP) at New York University's Tisch School of the Arts. As he built various projects during his studies, Chladil began to focus on how to keep his ideas more fluid throughout the process of creating work. He sought collaborations where he could contribute technical expertise and learn ways to sustain creative development.

Chladil's work at ITP culminated in the modular "rope&pulley" media control system he invented in order to combine the expressiveness and physicality of human gestures with the power and flexibility of digital media to create new multimedia performances. The projects flowing from this modular performance system encompass themes of reuse, emotional expression, and the cyclical nature of human experience. One of the projects allowed four participants to remix and improvise with independent tracks of music. Using loops of rope suspended from floor to ceiling, they could play their tracks forward, backward and at differing volumes to tailor the musical output to their liking.

As a recipient of a Digital Performance Institute residency, Chladil used the opportunity to develop a live performance using large drawing gestures to create synthesized soundscapes with the rope&pulley system. Ultimately, he built another media control prototype and he will be building new engaging performances that incorporate these systems.

Currently, Chladil is supporting the Emerging Media Technology program at the City University of New York. He also continues to partner with clients to develop working prototypes of hybrid hardware/ software systems and balances these activities with developing his own work.

michael.chladil@ropeandpulley.com
www.ropeandpulley.com

IMAGES

THE MAKING OF "OVERHEARD"

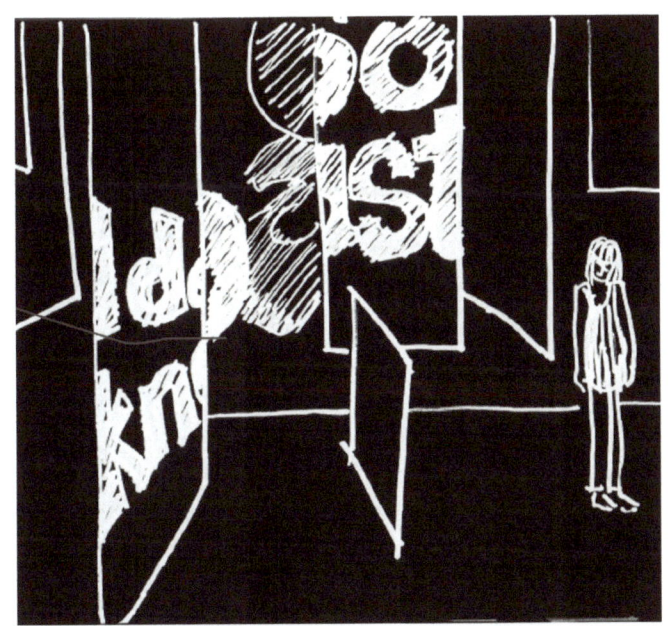

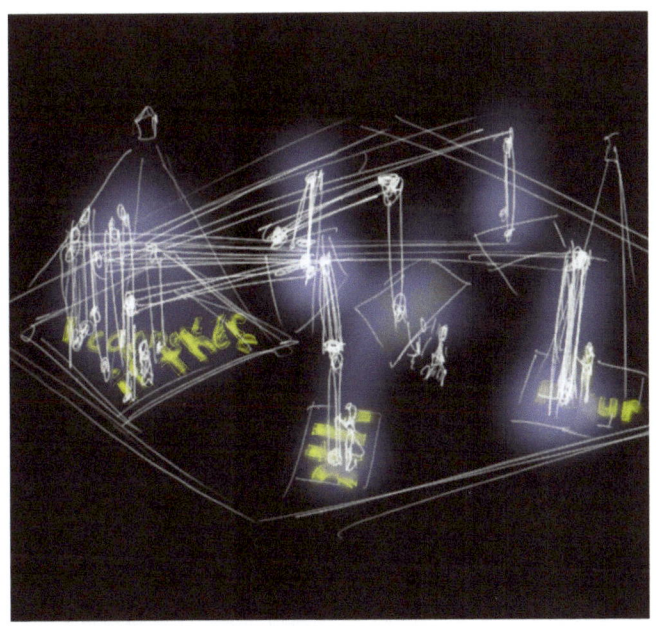

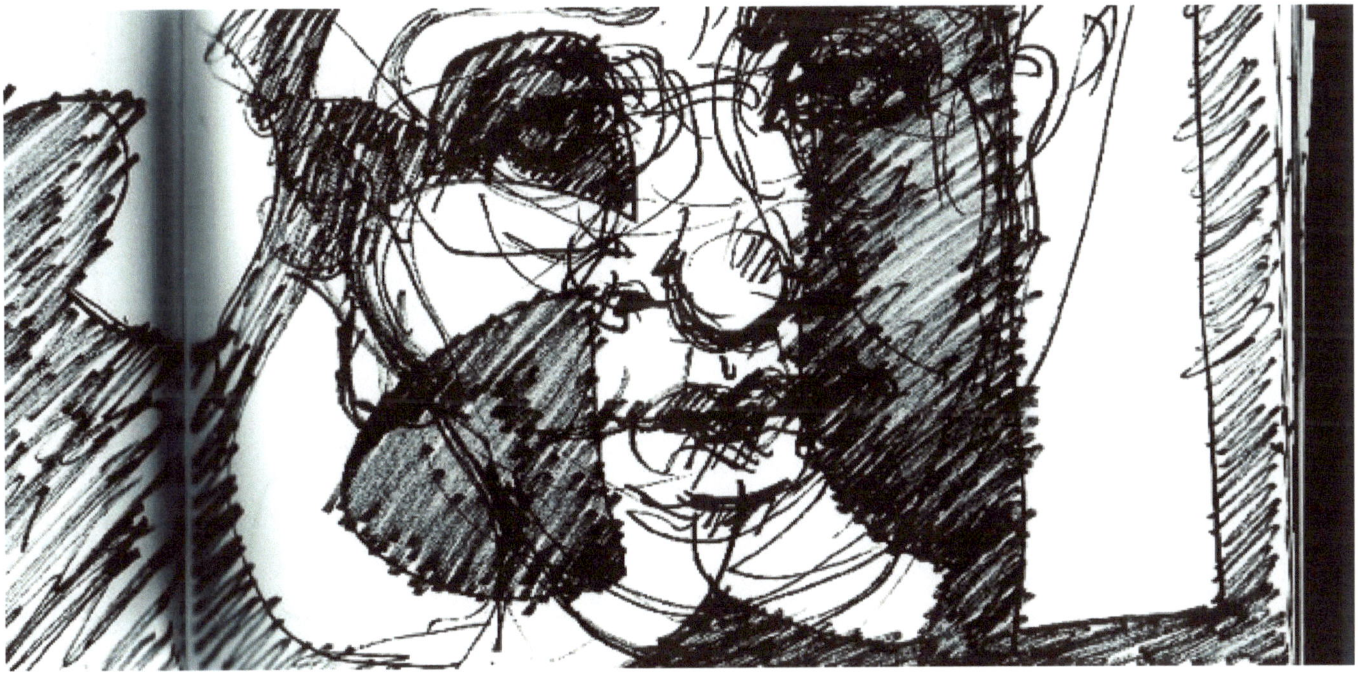

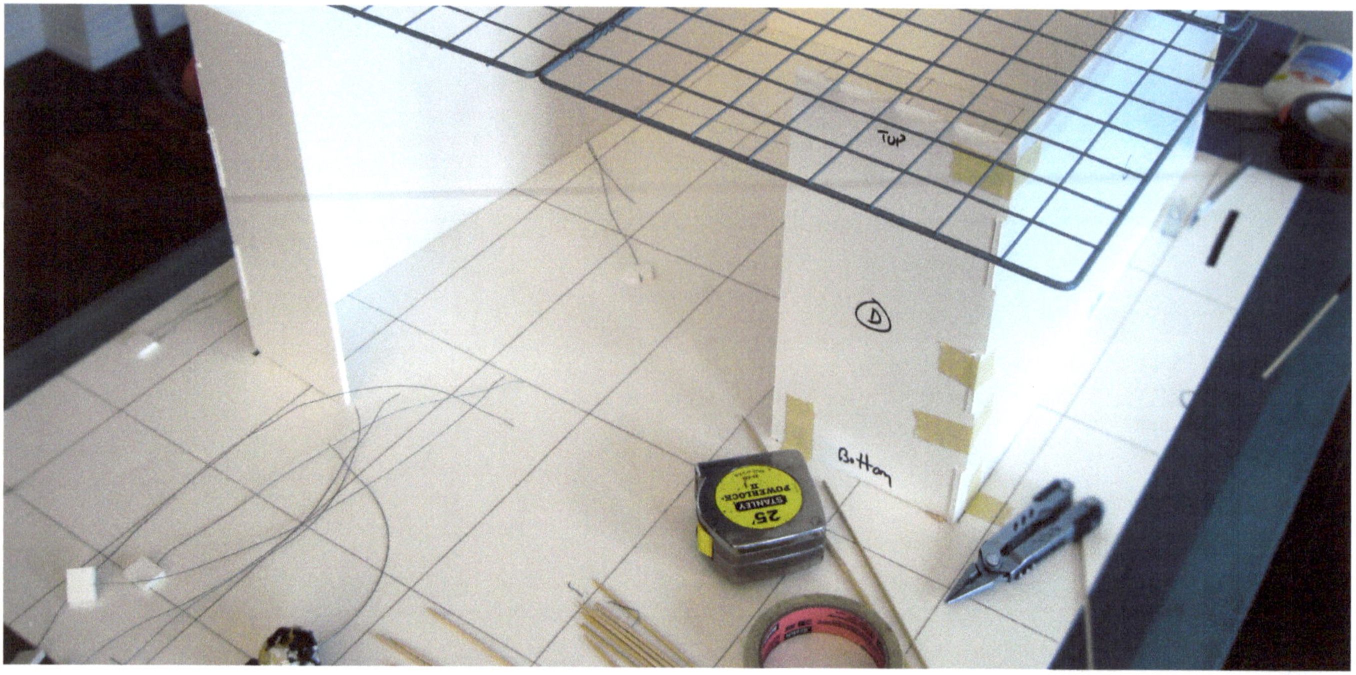

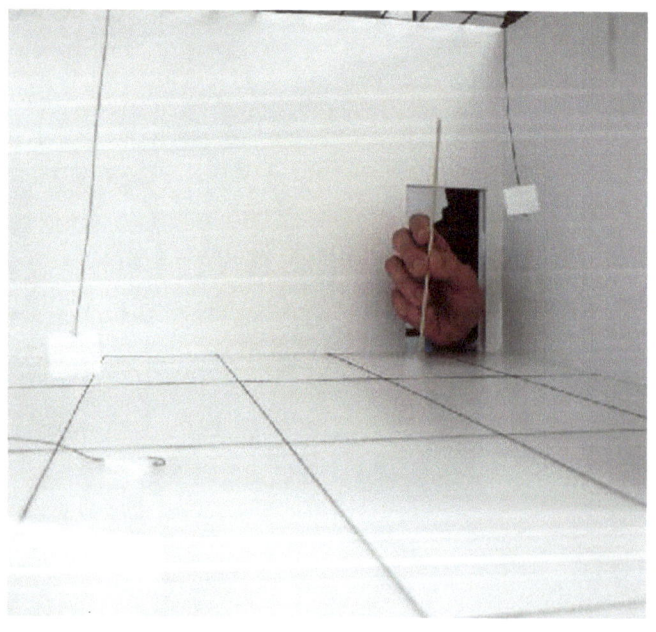

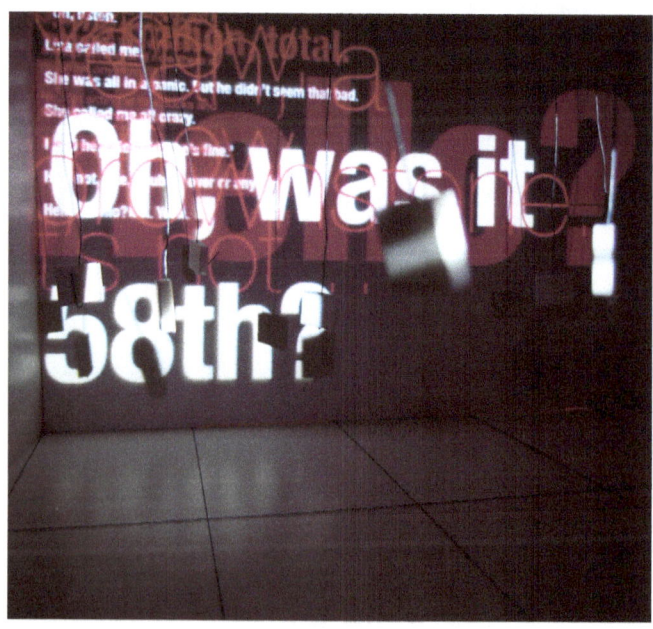

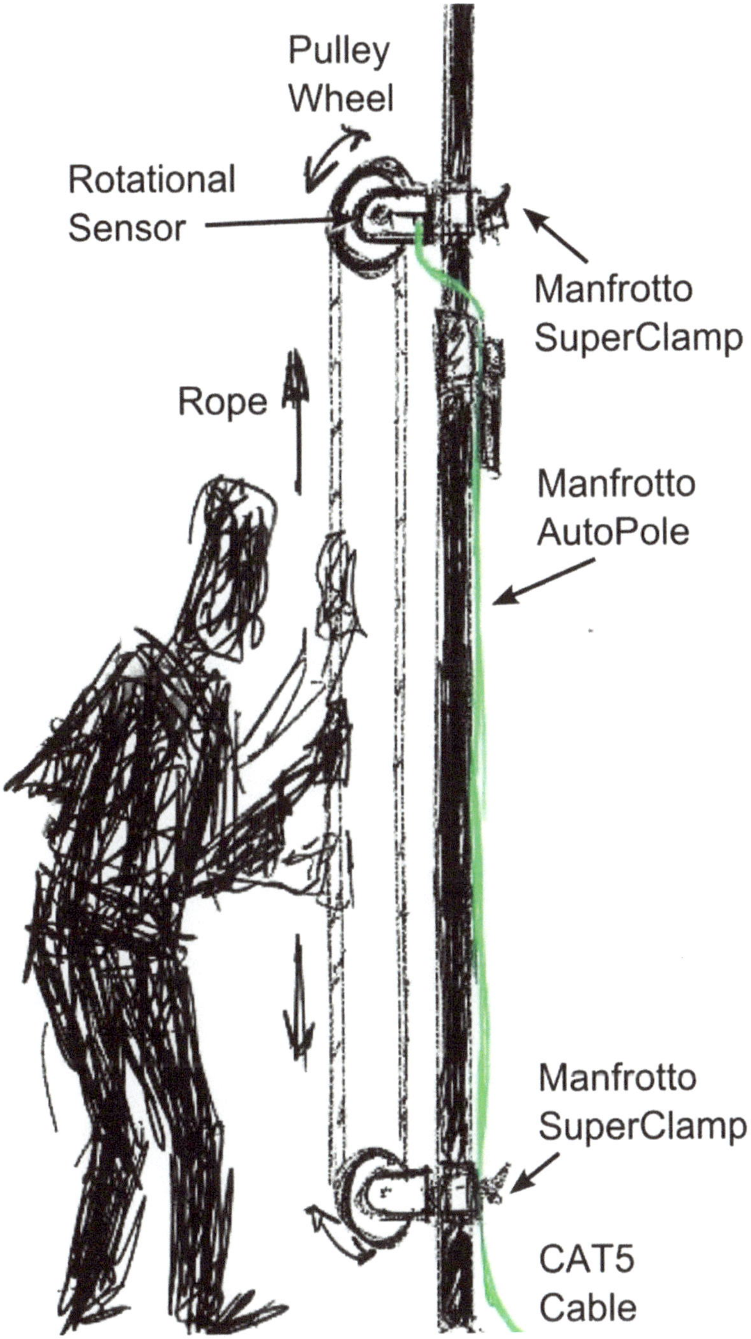

Pulley
Wheel

Rotational
Sensor

Rope

Manfrotto
SuperClamp

Manfrotto
AutoPole

Manfrotto
SuperClamp

CAT5
Cable

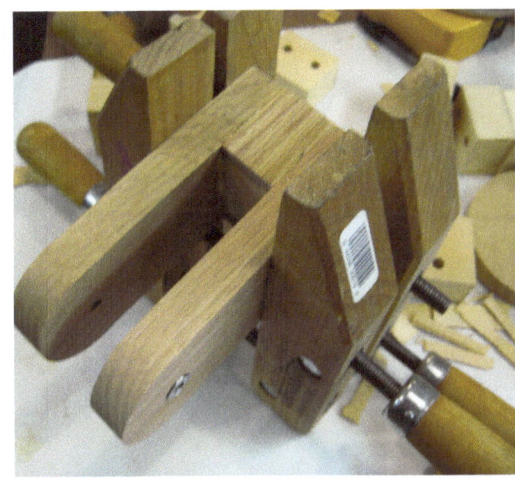

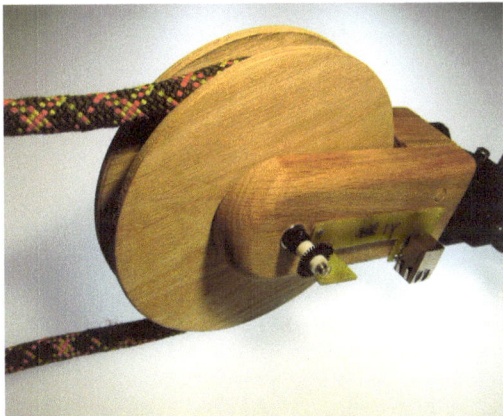

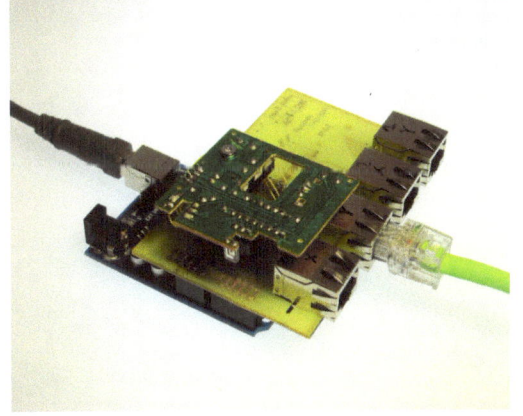

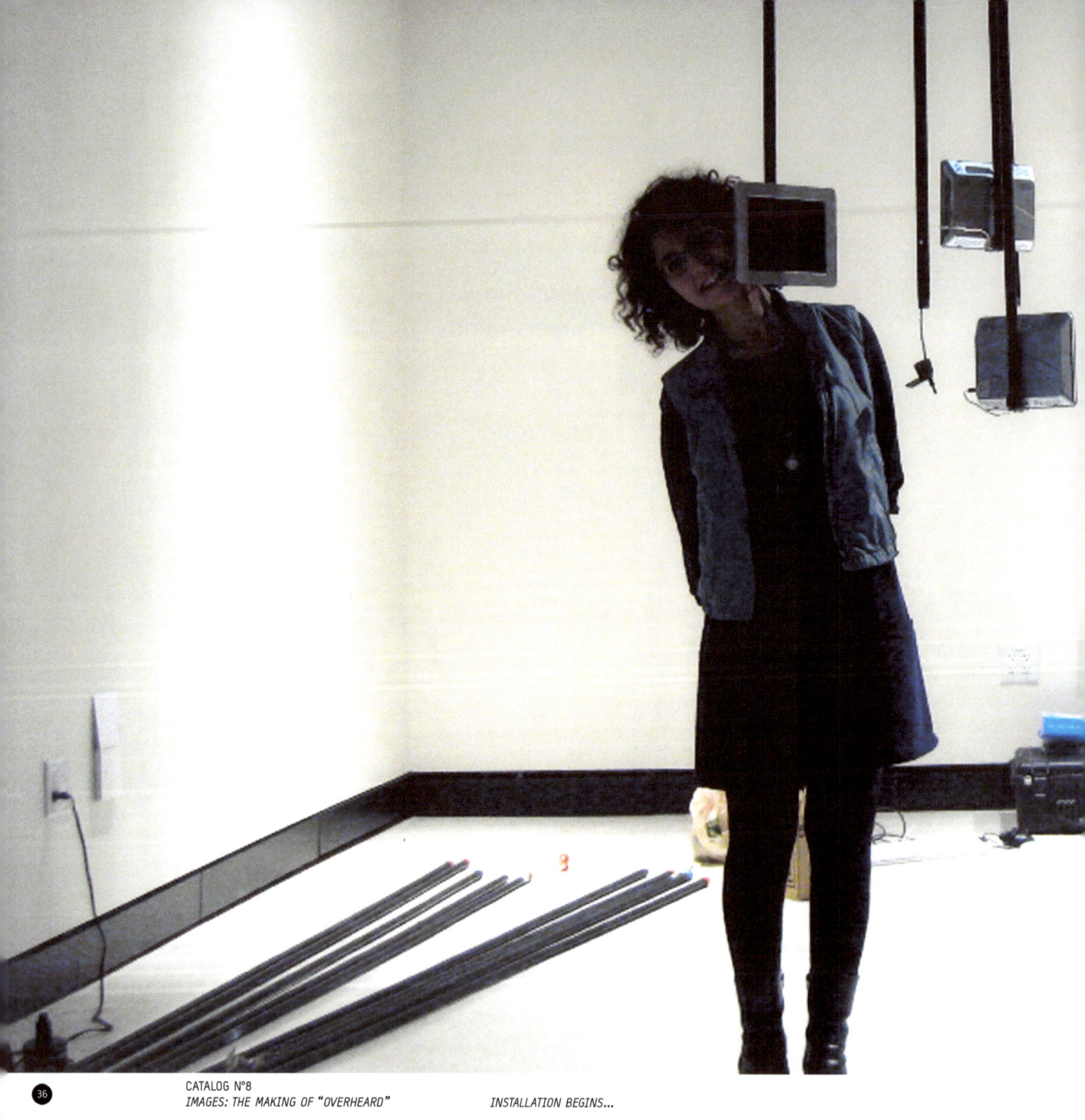

CATALOG N°8
IMAGES: THE MAKING OF "OVERHEARD"   *INSTALLATION BEGINS...*

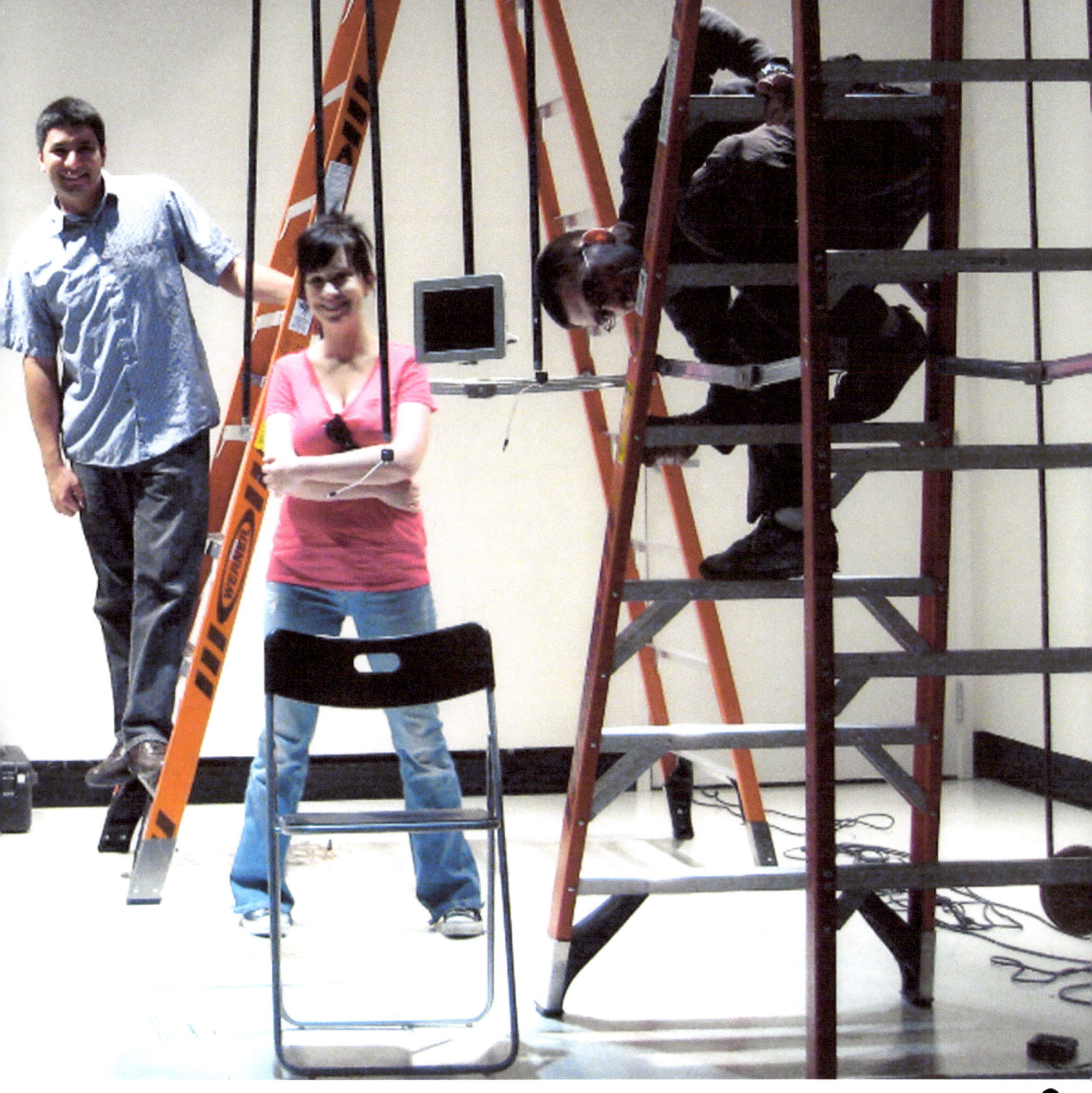

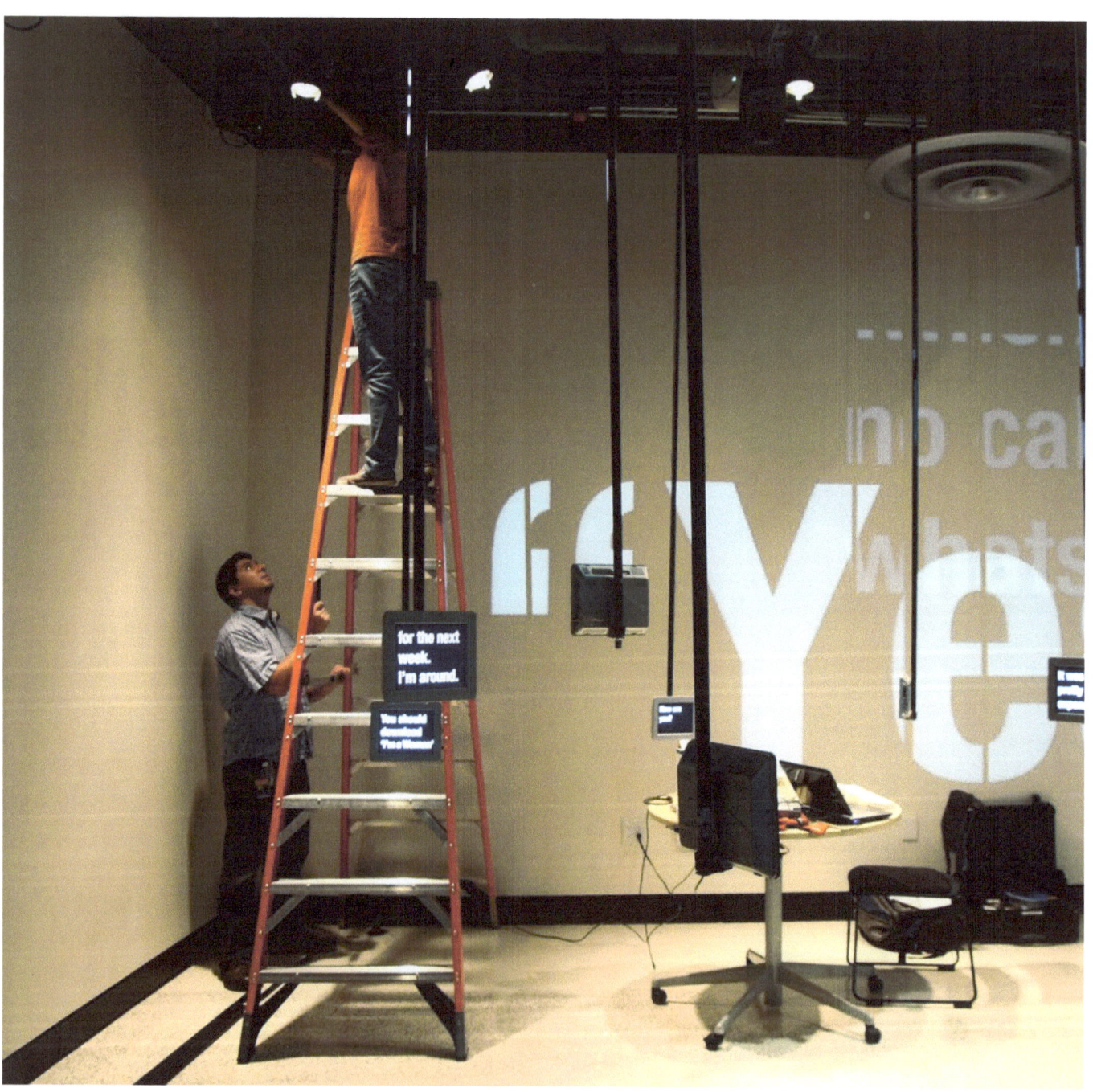

CATALOG Nº8
IMAGES: THE MAKING OF "OVERHEARD"

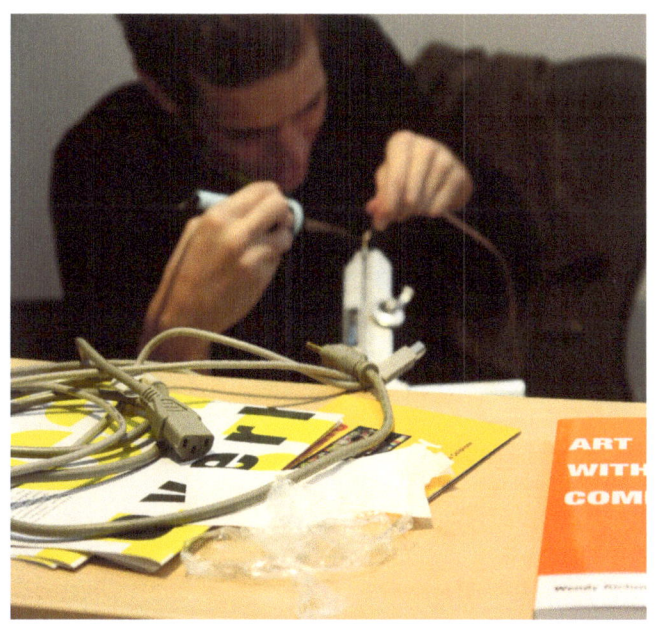

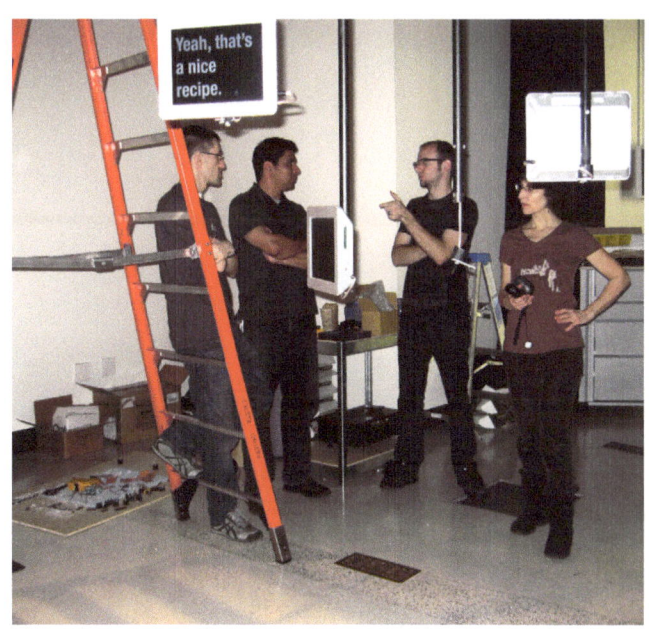

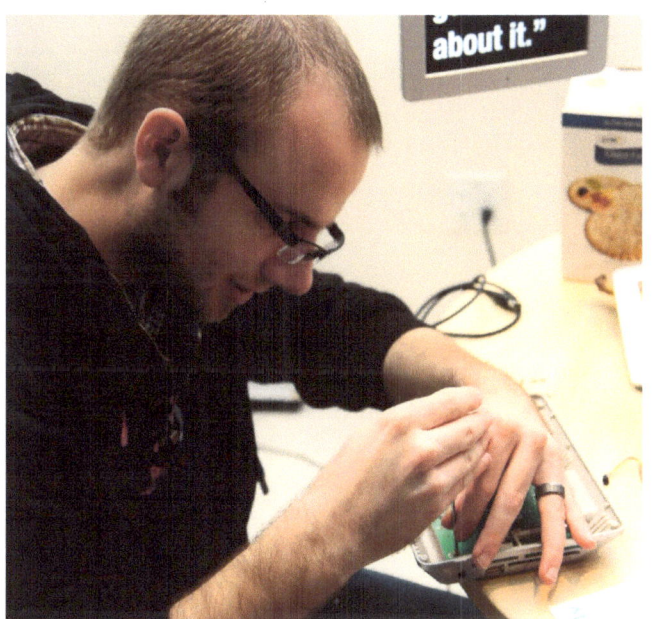

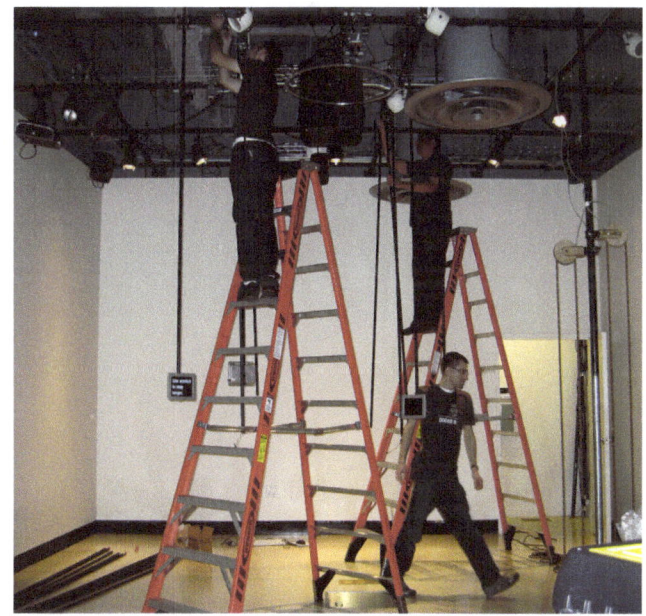

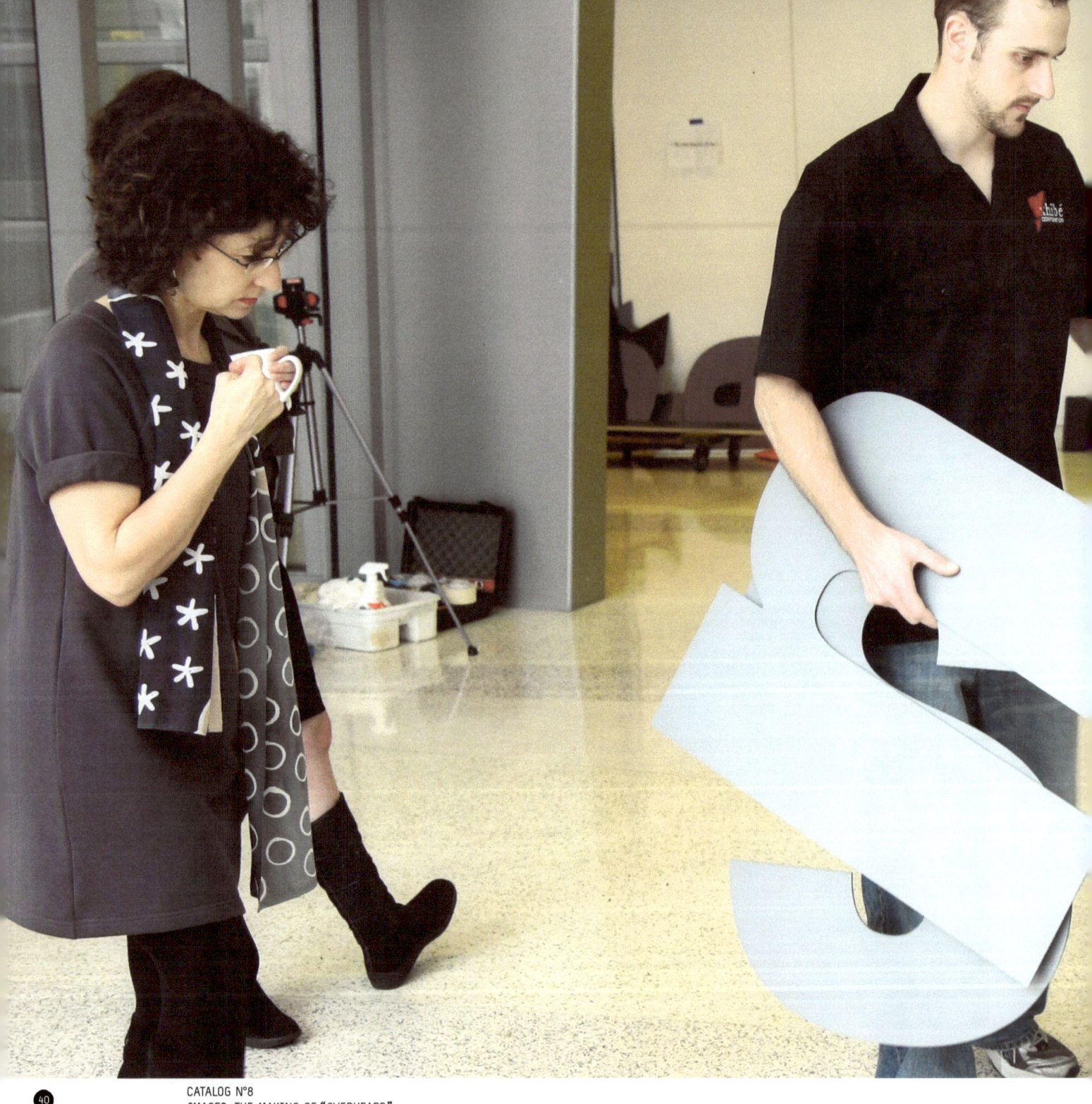

CATALOG N°8
IMAGES: THE MAKING OF "OVERHEARD"

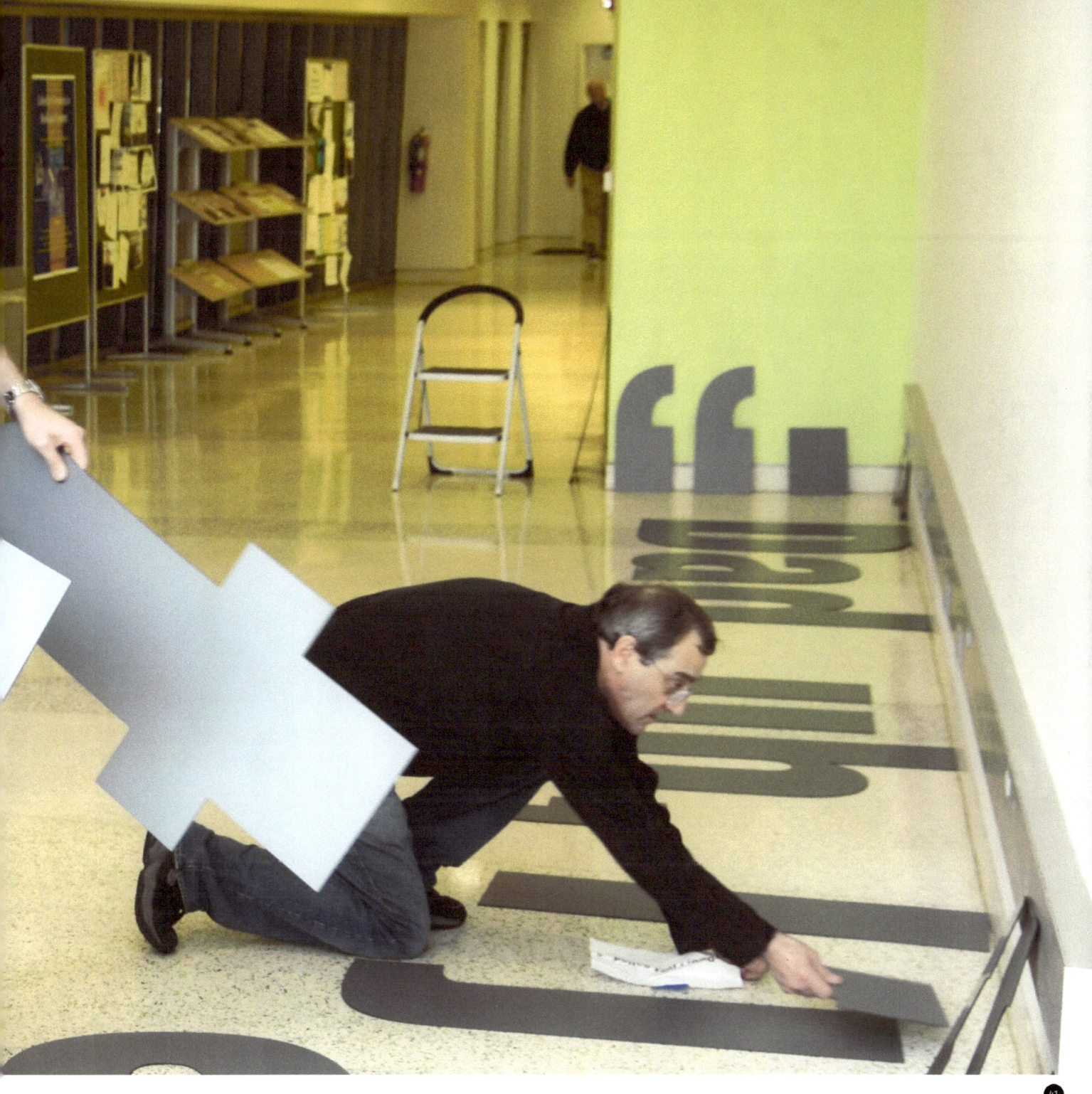

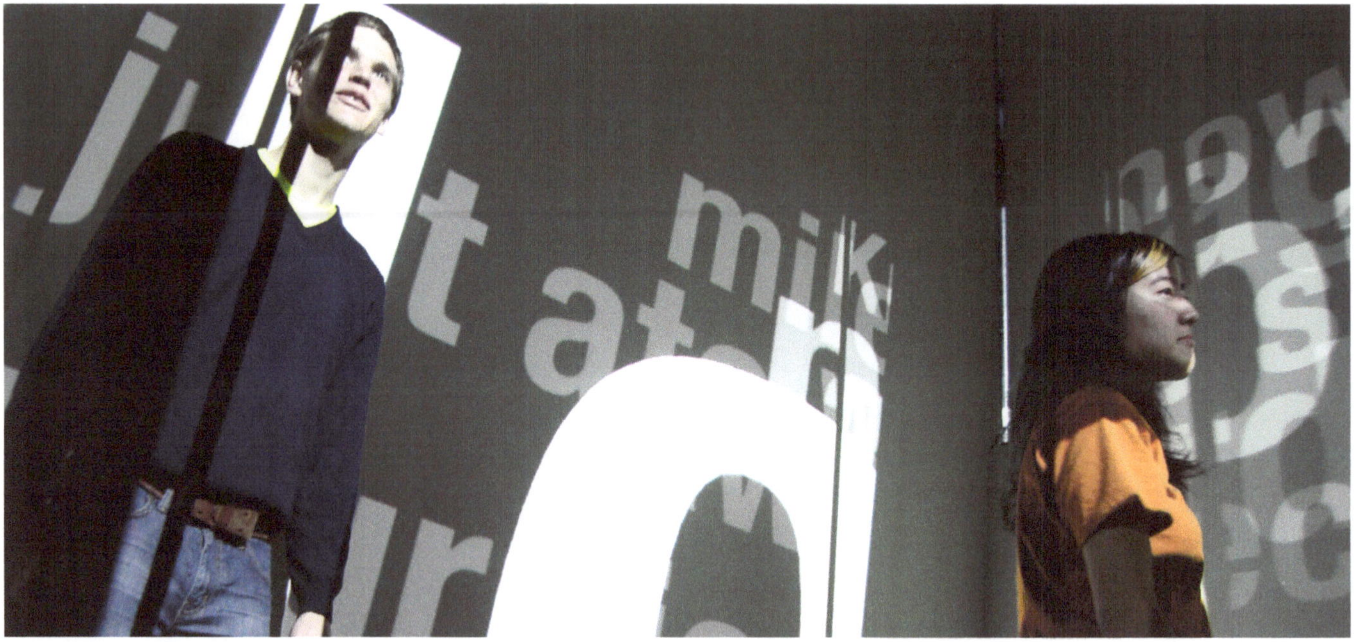

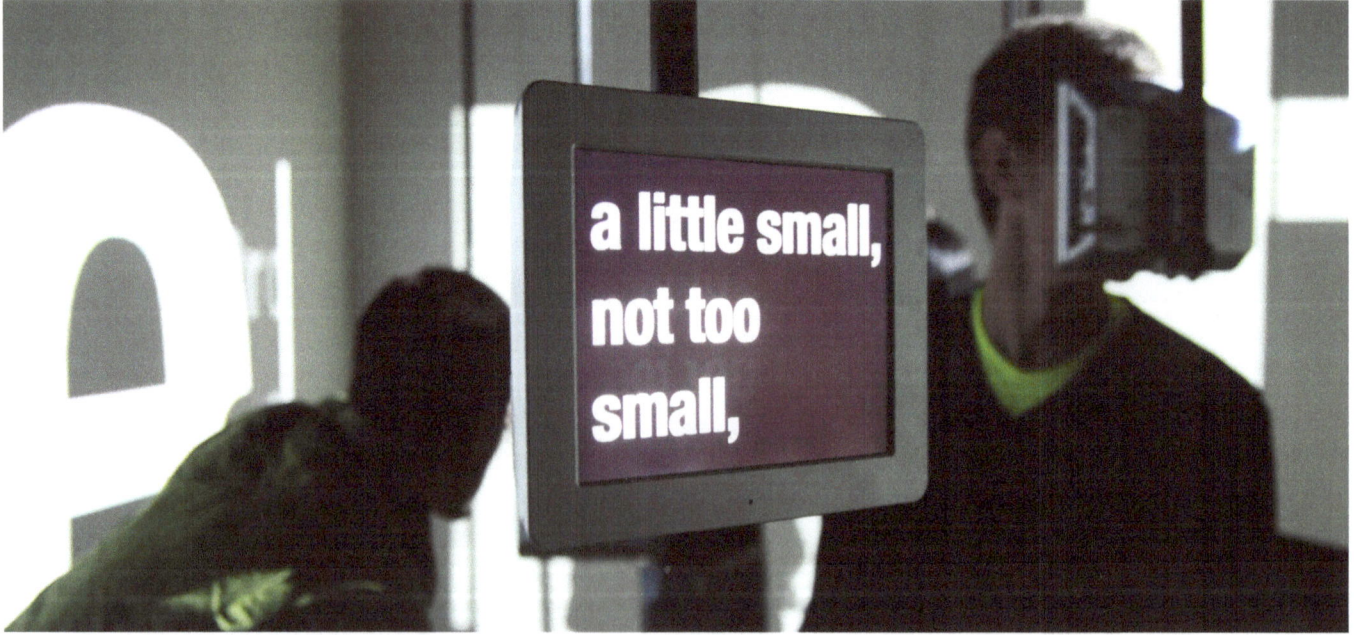

CATALOG N°8
IMAGES: THE MAKING OF "OVERHEARD"

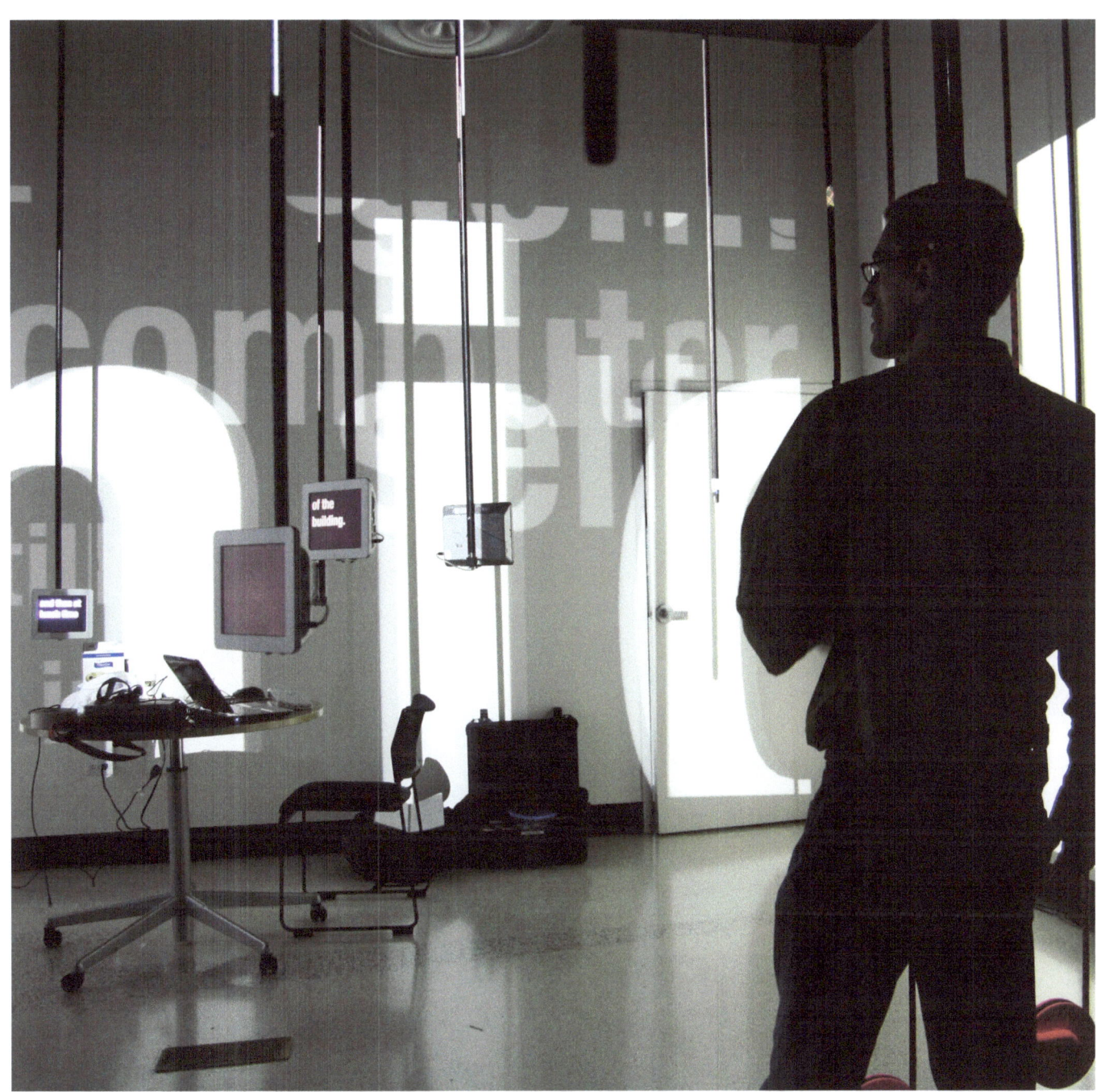

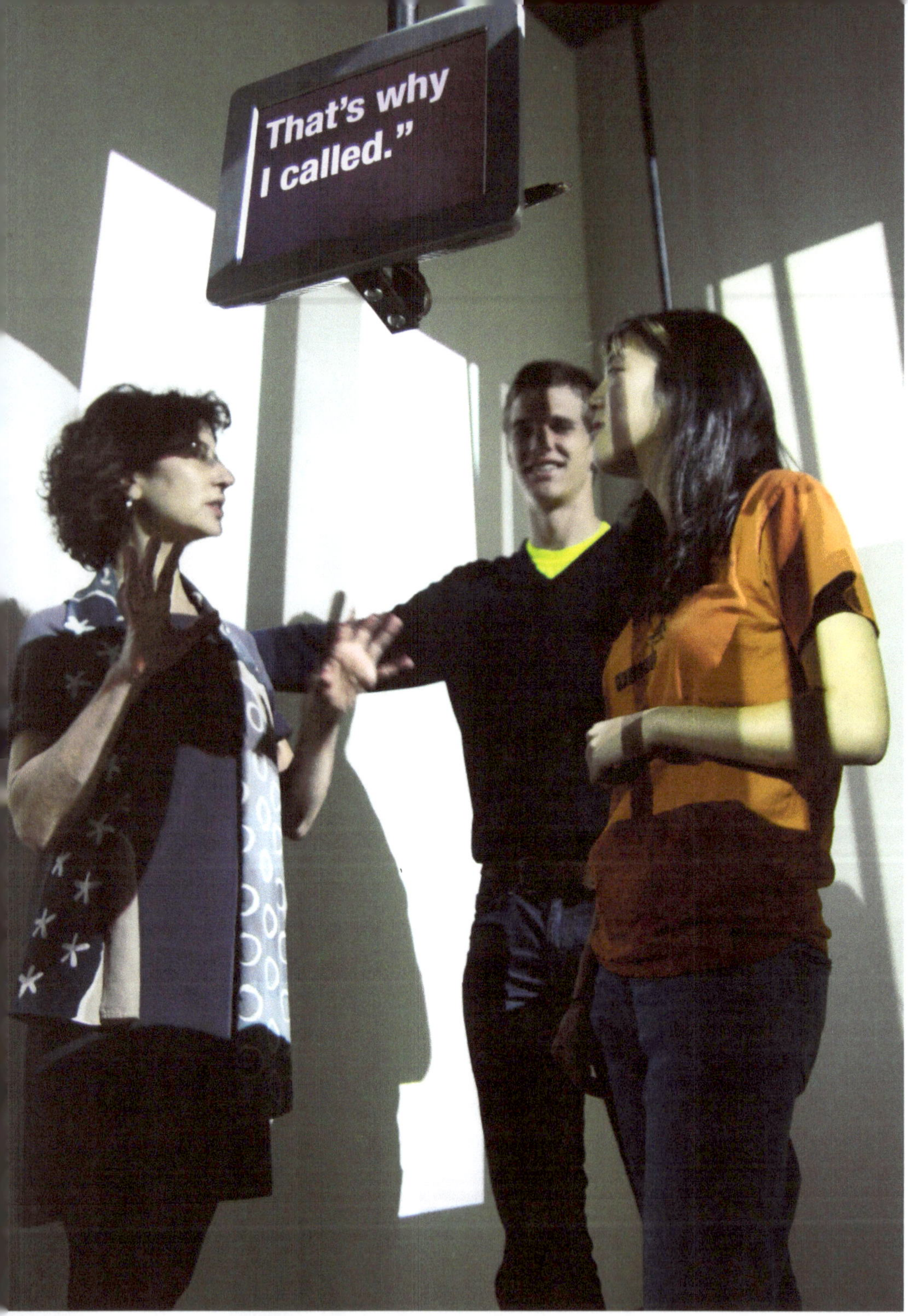

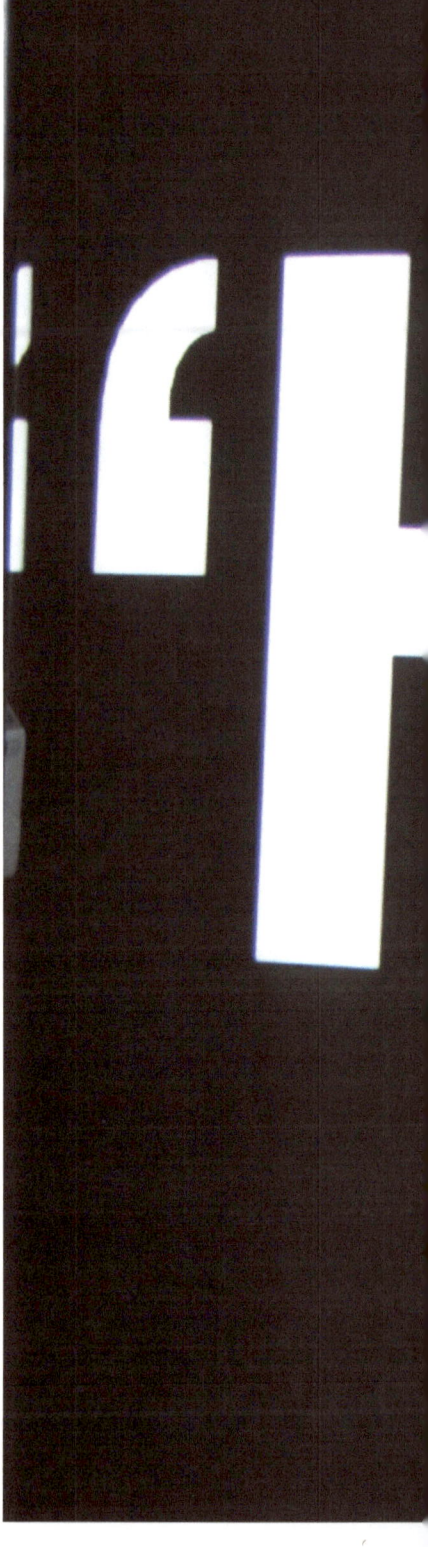

That's why
I called."

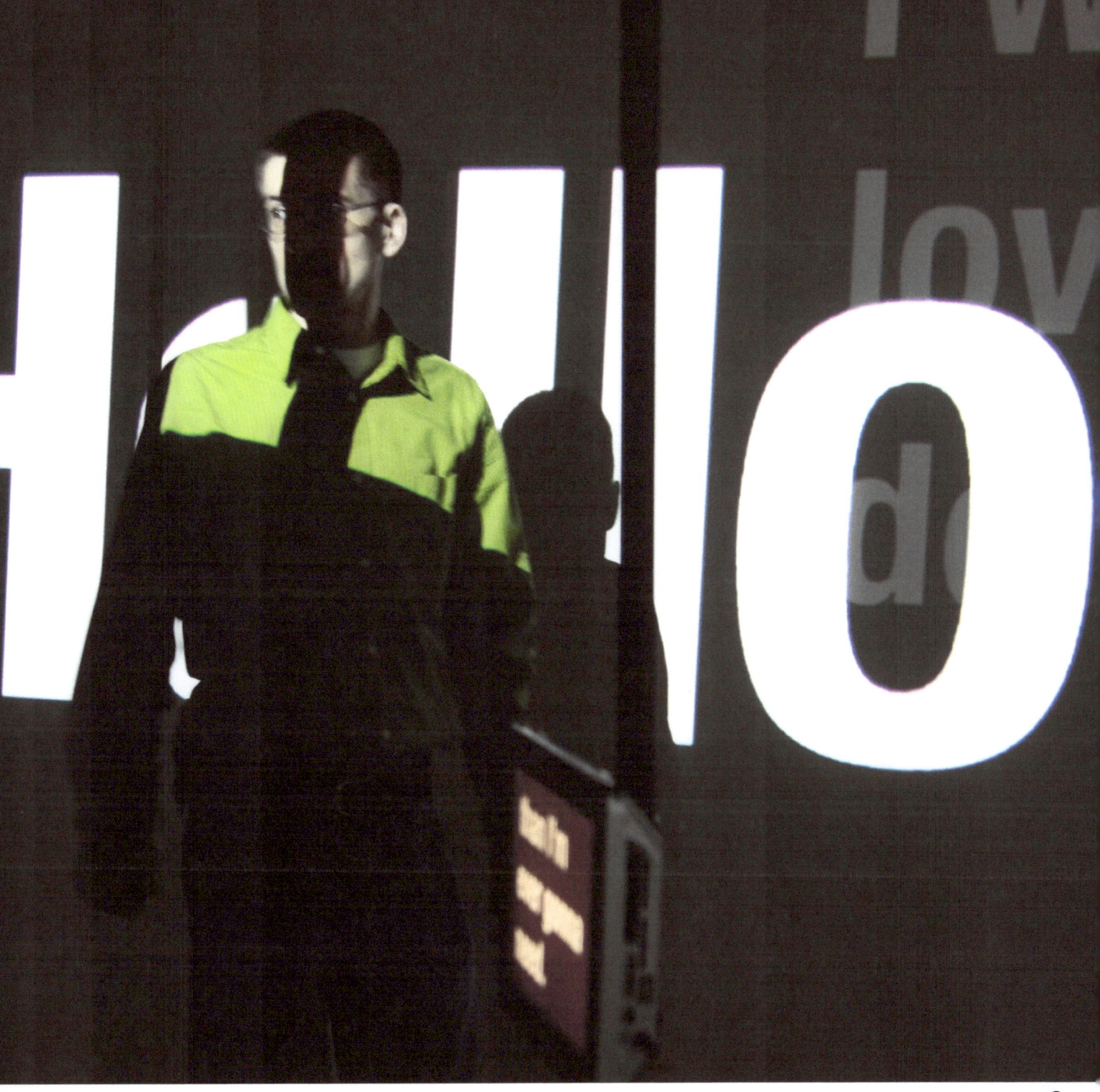

ACKNOWLEDGMENTS

A major theme in developing "Overheard" was to "Set up and let go," that is, to balance carefully constructed elements with a process of improvisation that would allow us to experience and refine the work. Our goal was to come to Calit2 with carefully designed elements: sound and visual content, software, and hardware; then, upon arrival, to let the work direct us.

To our great delight, we were supported in this endeavor throughout the entire project, from its original inception, development, set-up, and the creation of this catalog. Everyone who was involved in "Overheard" became a part of our collaboration.

The original impetus for showing this work at the University of California, San Diego came from the California Institute for Telecommunications and Information Technology (Calit2) and its director, Larry Smarr, as well as the co-chair of the gallery@calit2's faculty advisory committee, Lea Rudee, a former dean of the engineering school at UC San Diego. Calit2 is a place where engineers and computer scientists proactively engage with artists. It nurtures this collaboration by investing in its own art gallery. We are indebted to all at Calit2 for their expertise, passion and support in every detail.

From start to finish, gallery coordinator Trish Stone shepherded the show, working with us over many months to make it happen. Hector Bracho and his team in A/V services at Calit2, notably Adam Burruss, provided creative and expert technical support. They worked long hours to help us prepare for and set up the show, which required customized solutions. Thanks also go to Calit2's Cristian Horta for the layout and Doug Ramsey for editing this catalog; to Alexander Matthews for his videography; to Jonathan Lee for his photographic essay; and to Mark Plummer for administrative support at Calit2.

Our process of developing "Overheard" included many contributors. Thanks to the Digital Performance Institute – a laboratory for innovative performance technology – for the equipment we used during our experimentation (http://digitalperformance.org). We are also grateful to the DeBaun Auditorium at Stevens Institute of Technology for early experimentation space and pre-production support.

Our "prototype party," during which we showed work-in-progress, elicited valuable insights. Our thanks to our guests: Kelly Chladil, Susan Hodara, Paul Hodara, Sofie Hodara, DK Holland, Dennis Hromin, Mia Narell, Phil and Fran Mendlow, Joy Tomasko, and Meiyin Wang.

Our deep appreciation goes to Sofie Hodara for her drawings, design and production of the "Overheard" cups, and to Susan Hodara for interviewing us for this catalog. Thanks also to David Liatti / Glide Design for fabrication assistance, to Exhibé Corporation (www.exhibe.com) for the large-scale wall lettering, and to Sara Guttman and Edge Studio (www.edgestudio.com) for recording voice actors including Lisa Adams, Ami Kozak, Mick Lauer, Cathy Mancuso, Danielle Quisenberry, Noelle Romano, and Joey Schaljo. Other recorded voices belong to Timothy Dalton, Stacy Davidowitz, Karen Grenke, Henri Hodara, Sofie Hodara, Frank Ishman, Pedro Jimenez, April Sweeney and James "Face" Yu.

Finally we want to thank the entire Hodara family and Michael's wife Kelly for their continuing support and encouragement.

– Wendy Richmond and Michael Chladil

gallery@calit2 reflects the nexus of innovation implicit in Calit2's vision, and aims to advance our understanding and appreciation of the dynamic interplay among art, science and technology.

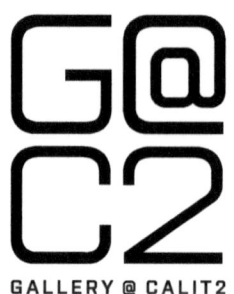

GALLERY @ CALIT2

First Floor
Atkinson Hall
9500 Gilman Drive
University of California, San Diego
La Jolla, CA 92093

http://gallery.calit2.net

www.ingramcontent.com/pod-product-compliance
Lightning Source LLC
Chambersburg PA
CBHW051058180526
45172CB00002B/689